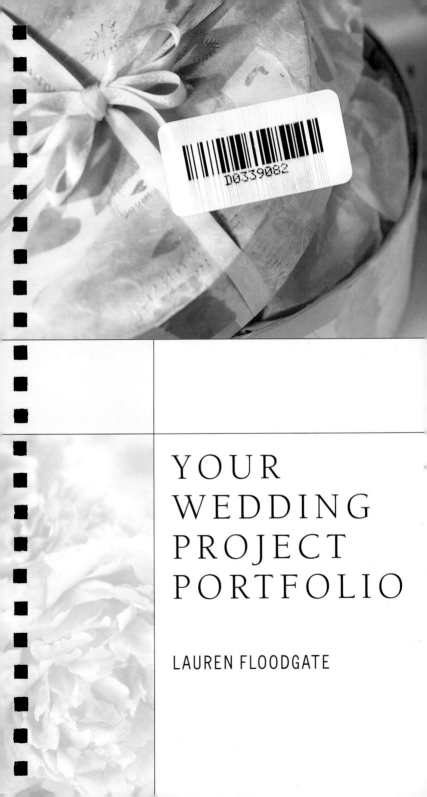

# YOUR WEDDING PROJECT PORTFOLIO

LAUREN FLOODGATE

# CONTENTS

# DEDICATION

This book is dedicated to my husband Richard for his enthusiasm and support.

# INTRODUCTION

You've just got engaged and the following months will culminate in what will be one of the most romantic and memorable days of your life. Once you have made the decision about the style of wedding that you want, you then have to bring your ideas to life. So where to begin? With this book you will have everything at hand to make your wedding a personal and special day that your friends and family will all treasure.

*Your Wedding Project Portfolio* is designed to help you create the dream wedding day.

Whether you only make a simple veil or embark on a more ambitious task, such as creating you own flower arrangements, the beauty is that you will know the item is unique and all your own work. It is also a good opportunity to get family and friends involved—a great way to spend time with those that are close to you in the days leading up to the wedding. No detail is too small to be overlooked, in fact it's the details that guests will remember; the handmade stationery, the beautiful table centerpiece, the delicate favors, it's all these special touches that will make your wedding day so memorable.

Designed with the busy person in mind, I've tried to take away as much of the hard work as possible. The projects are beautiful, inspiring, and simple to make. The step-by-step text is easy to follow and is accompanied by illustrations and a full-color photograph. Key items such as the bridal headdresses, bouquets, table centerpieces, and wedding invitations have been created in four styles—traditional, modern, romantic, and country. This means that you can follow a theme to create a coordinated look. Dip in and out of this book, follow it exactly, or use it to simply inspire your own creativity. No matter what path you choose, *Your Wedding Project Portfolio* will undoubtedly help you to create a wedding that is truly your own.

# HINTS AND SAFETY GUIDELINES

► Before starting any of the projects read through the instructions and make sure that you understand what you are being asked to do. Be patient. You'll get much better results if you take your time.

► Prepare a work surface. You should make sure that any surfaces that may get scratched or damaged are covered with a cloth or newspaper etc. to protect them.

► When using any products such as glues, paints, varnishes, electrical appliances etc. you should always follow the manufacturer's instructions.

► If you are using a product that you've never used before or a technique that you're not familiar with, try it out first on a small piece of the material that you will be using, before starting work on the whole item.

► Take great care when cutting materials with a craft knife. You should always use a cutting mat.

► When using spray paints or varnishes, follow the manufacturer's instructions carefully. You should work in a well-ventilated room or outside.

► Any item involving the use of fresh flowers should not be made earlier than the morning of the wedding if it is to look its best. Lightly mist the finished item with water and keep in a cool place. However, fresh flower items should never be kept in the refrigerator. If it is a tied bouquet the stems can be kept in water.

► Lit candles should not be left unattended.

*bride*

**and bridal party**

# BEADED VEIL

## YOU WILL NEED

- ▶ Paper
- ▶ Scissors
- ▶ 8 feet white or ivory bridal netting, 6-feet wide
- ▶ Pins
- ▶ Needle
- ▶ Gold or silver sewing thread, or a color that matches your dress
- ▶ At least 100 small pearl beads
- ▶ Tweezers
- ▶ All-purpose clear drying-glue
- ▶ White or ivory sewing thread
- ▶ Clear hair comb

▲ Enlarge the veil pattern on page 118. Transfer to a large sheet of paper and cut out. Fold the pattern and netting in half lengthwise. Lay the pattern on the net, aligning the folds. Pin in place and cut out. Repeat three or four times. You will have separate extended semicircles of netting.

► Thread the needle with your chosen thread and carefully sew along the outside edge of one of the semicircles of netting to give the veil a weighted, colored edge. Use running stitches, keeping the stitches as small and as close to the edge as possible. Repeat with the remaining nets.

◄ Spread one of the nets out on a clean work surface and put the beads in a container. Pick a bead up using the tweezers, dab with a little glue, and position on the netting either randomly or following a chosen pattern. Continue gluing beads to the net keeping them evenly spaced apart and applying as little glue as possible. Allow to dry.

► Double thread the needle with thread that matches the color of the netting. Lay the three semicircles of net one on top of the other with the beaded net on top, bead-side up. Pin in place along the straight edge. Tie a large knot in the end of the sewing thread and stitch along the straight edge of the nets, stitching through all thicknesses, and keeping the stitches within ¼ inch of the edge of the netting, and to about 1 inch in length. Pull the threads gently to gather up the veiling, pulling until the gathered length of netting is as long as the width of the comb. Secure the gathers with a few small stitches, and then carefully stitch the gathered netting to the top of the comb using as few stitches as possible. The veil is very light so only a few unobtrusive stitches will be necessary; however, make sure there is enough stitching so that the netting is securely attached to the comb.

## ROMANTIC
# ROSE CIRCLET

### YOU WILL NEED

- ▶ Tape measure
- ▶ Twelve red rosebuds
- ▶ Scissors
- ▶ Twelve 6-inch lengths of medium-gauge florist's wire
- ▶ Florist's tape
- ▶ Hypericum berries
- ▶ Small-leafed green foliage
- ▶ Eight to ten lengths of small-leafed ivy and berries, at least 4 inches long

▶ ▼ Measure the circumference of the crown of your head and make a note of the measurement as this will be the length of the circlet. Cut the stems from the roses to just beneath the calyxes. Thread 2 inches of a 6-inch length of wire through the widest part of the calyx of one rose, twist the ends of the wire together beneath the calyx and then wrap a little florist's tape around the calyx and twisted wires to secure. As you wrap the tape, pull it taut and stretch it slightly. Repeat with the remaining rosebuds and set aside.

► Cut the foliage and ivy into manageable lengths, about 3 to 4 inches long, and the stems of the hypericum and berries to about 1 inch beneath the berry heads.

▼ Take a wired rosebud in your left hand, hold a little greenery and ivy beneath it, and start wrapping the florist's tape down the wire of the rose, pulling the tape tightly and binding the greenery to the wire as you wrap. Continue wrapping in this way, adding tightly packed berries, greenery, and roses. Keep the stems pointing in the same direction with the leaves facing upward. Keep the circlet quite dense to give it strength and continue until it is as long as your head measurement.

► Join the ends of the circlet together and finish off. Secure with tape. Lightly mist with water and keep cool.

# RIBBON ROSE CLIP

## YOU WILL NEED

► Four 14-inch lengths of 3-inch wide wired ribbon in coordinating colors

► 3-inch long hairclip

► Coordinating sewing thread

► Needle

► Scissors

► All-purpose glue or hot glue gun

▲ Iron the ribbons and fold in half lengthwise. Hold the end of one of the ribbons between the thumb and forefinger of your left hand, folded edge pointing upward.

► Wrap the ribbon behind the forefinger, over the thumb and then over the third finger. Wrap the ribbon behind the third finger and then over your fourth finger. Continue wrapping over your thumb and third finger.

► Using your right hand, pinch the ribbon together at the fingertips of your left hand and then carefully slide the ribbon off the fingers. You will now have a rose shape. Carefully stitch the base of the rose together to hold the ribbon in place. Repeat to make four roses.

▼ ◄ You can stitch the roses to the hairclip but it is easier to glue them in place. If sewing, open the clip and take the thread through the ribbon rose and around the upper arm of the clip. To insure the roses do not slip, dot a little glue under each before sewing. To glue, dot glue along the upper arm of the clip and press the base of each rose firmly onto the glue. Hold until secure and leave to set. When the glue is dry, trim any frayed ends and then carefully ease open each rose so they are all evenly sized and the hair clip is completely covered.

## YOU WILL NEED

- ► Silver-colored hairband
- ► Ruler
- ► Spool of medium-weight silver beading wire
- ► Scissors
- ► Fifteen 5-millimeter diameter turquoise glass beads
- ► Pliers
- ► One hundred 2-millimeter diameter clear glass beads
- ► One hundred 2-millimeter diameter medium-blue glass beads
- ► Eighty 5-millimeter long silver-centered clear tube beads
- ► Sixty 3-millimeter diameter pearl-effect beads
- ► Sixty 4-millimeter diameter clear glass beads

MODERN

# BLUE AND SILVER GLASS TIARA

◄ Mark the middle of the hairband. Measure 1 inch on either side of the center and make a second set of marks, points 1 and 2.

► Cut the following lengths of wire; two pieces at 7-inches, four pieces at 6-inches, eight pieces at 5-inches, and eight pieces at 4-inches.

▼ Thread a large turquoise bead to the center of one of the 7-inch lengths of wire. Hold the other 7-inch length alongside the first wire. Using the pliers, twist the wires together on either side of the bead. Continue twisting the wires on one side of the bead for approximately 1 inch and then thread two small clear glass beads onto one of the wires. Continue twisting the wires until you reach the end. Repeat this process on the other side of the turquoise bead. This piece of wire is the centerpiece of the tiara. Wrap one end of this twisted wire twice around the hairband at point 1. Wrap the other end around the band at point 2. You will now have a neat semi-circular loop. Trim off any sharp ends of wire.

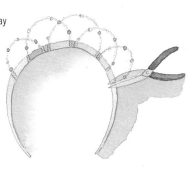

▶ Make 10 more wire loops in the same way but it is important to vary the number and color of the beads on each wire to give the tiara its natural, unsymmetrical feel. Attach a second 6-inch twisted wire, one end of the wire at the mid-point of the hairband and the other end 1 inch from point 1. Do the same with the third wire but this time secure it at the mid-point and 1 inch from point 2. Continue adding beaded twisted wires, overlapping and interweaving them as you go until you have a tiara decorated with loops that decrease in size as they radiate outward.

Cut a 20-inch length of wire and loop a knot in one end. Randomly thread on all the remaining beads. If your hairband has a small hole at either end, thread the unknotted end of the wire through one hole and then wrap around the band several times to secure. If it doesn't, attach the wire ½ inch in from one end of the band. Slide the beads to the end of the wire attached to the band and start wrapping it around the hairband making sure that one to three beads are positioned at the front of the band with each wrap of the wire. To give the tiara a rich encrusted look, make sure there are plenty of beads between the ends of each loop of twisted wire. This final wire is to decorate the band and hide any loose ends of wire or unsightly joins, so don't try and wrap the wire too neatly or too tightly. Secure at the other hole or with a few tight winds of wire and then cut off any loose ends. Carefully try on the tiara for comfort. If any ends of wire are sharp give them a squeeze with the pliers to flatten.

# BRIDESMAID'S BALLET SLIPPERS

## YOU WILL NEED

▶ Satin ballet slippers

▶ Tissue paper

▶ Silk paint in the color of your choice

▶ One large and one small artist's paintbrush

▶ Hairdryer

▶ Selection of small silk flowers and leaves

▶ Scissors

▶ All-purpose glue or a hot-melt glue gun

▶ Stuff the ballet slippers with the tissue paper, easing out any large creases or folds; the better the shape the more evenly the slippers will dye. Before you start dyeing check the silk paint is the correct color by painting a little on the underside of one of the slippers and allowing it to dry. It is important that the paint is allowed to dry before proceeding because some paints change color as they dry, ending up considerably lighter or darker. If the paint is the color you want, continue; if not, buy another color and repeat the test or lighten the color with a silk paint diluent.

▲ Put a little paint into a small container and beginning at the front, work towards the back, painting the slippers with long strokes. Apply enough paint to cover the slippers sufficiently, but do not saturate the fabric otherwise the paint may bleed into the lining. Apply another coat if a deeper shade is required.

Remove the paper stuffing. Heat-fix the paint using a hairdryer set to high. Blow-dry the slippers until they are completely dry. This will fix the paint sufficiently for the slippers to be worn on a dry day. Care must be taken to keep the slippers from getting wet as otherwise they may stain the feet or items of clothing.

▲ Pull the silk flowers from the stems and trim away the plastic at the back. Cut the leaves down to the appropriate size. Arrange the flowers and leaves as they are to appear on the slippers. When you are happy with the design stick them to the front of the slippers . Allow to dry thoroughly before wearing.

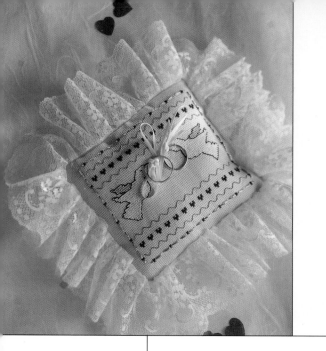

## YOU WILL NEED

► 10-inch square piece of cross-stitch fabric
► Six-stranded embroidery threads in seven different colors (red, blue, silver, gray, white, black, and yellow)
► Embroidery needle
► Small embroidery hoop
► Scissors
► Iron
► Two 6-inch lengths of cream ribbon
► Needle and basting thread
► 4 feet of pale cream lace, 3-inches wide
► Pins
► Sewing machine
► 10-inch square medium-weight, cream fabric
► Wadding

# RING BEARER'S PILLOW

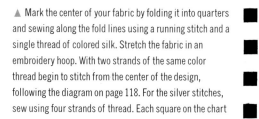

▲ Mark the center of your fabric by folding it into quarters and sewing along the fold lines using a running stitch and a single thread of colored silk. Stretch the fabric in an embroidery hoop. With two strands of the same color thread begin to stitch from the center of the design, following the diagram on page 118. For the silver stitches, sew using four strands of thread. Each square on the chart represents a single cross-stitch. To start, bring the embroidery needle up through a hole in the fabric, then across and down to form a diagonal stitch. Then work a second diagonal stitch on top to make a single cross. To work a row of cross-stitches, first make a row of diagonal stitches working from left to right and then complete by going back along the row to make crosses.

▶ Once you have finished, fasten and snip off the ends and remove the basting stitches. Iron on the reverse side. Sew a length of ribbon to the beak of each dove, then trim the cross-stitch fabric down to within 2 inches of the edge of the design.

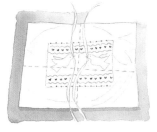

▶ Tie a knot in the end of a length of basting thread and sew a line of tacking stitches along the straight edge of the lace. Pull the thread gently until the gathered piece of lace measures approximately 19 inches. Sew a few stitches at each end of the gathers to secure. Pin the lace around the edge of the pillow so that the straight edge is 1 inch from the edge of the cross-stitch fabric and the fancy edge is facing inward. Baste in place and then hand-sew the two loose ends together.

Using a long straight stitch, machine-stitch the lace in place. Remove the basting stitches. Lay the pillow on the work surface, right side up with the lace still laying inward. Pin the cream square of fabric on top, baste in place, then remove the pins. Turn the work over and machine stitch along the existing line of stitching but stop sewing 3 inches from where you began. Trim away excess fabric and clip corners, then turn the pillow right-side out.

◀ Lightly stuff the pillow with wadding so it is plump and has a nice domed shape, then turn under the raw edges of the gap and slip-stitch in place.

# DECORATED SHOE CLIP

YOUR WEDDING PROJECT PORTFOLIO

## YOU WILL NEED

- ▶ Pair of ready-to-decorate shoe clips
- ▶ Newspaper
- ▶ Metallic silver spray paint (optional)
- ▶ All-purpose, clear glue
- ▶ Tweezers
- ▶ Selection of small glass or plastic beads in colors of your choice
- ▶ Silver relief paint
- ▶ Small paintbrush
- ▶ Moist cloth

▲ Most ready-to-decorate shoe clips are gold in color so if you require silver decorations you will need to spray them. Place the shoe clips on a sheet of newspaper in a well-ventilated room or outside. Use the paint according to the can instructions and give the clips two to three light coats of paint—allowing them to dry thoroughly between coats.

▼ ◄ If you wish, sketch out your design first, then arrange the beads in your chosen design on the work surface. Or, roughly position the largest beads on the clip to make sure that you are basically happy with the overall look. Thinly spread glue over the area of the shoe clip that is to be decorated.

◄ Put the largest beads into place and press down gently so they are firmly glued in place. Fill in the gaps with the medium-sized beads and finish with the smallest beads. The glue remains workable for some minutes so if a bead is in the wrong place or moves slightly, just remove it, wipe off the surplus glue, and reposition. Don't worry about filling up the entire area of the clip with beads as any small areas can be filled with relief paint.

When the glue has dried, carefully use relief paint to fill in any small holes or undecorated areas. Wipe away any excess paint with the corner of a moist cloth and allow the shoe clips to dry overnight.

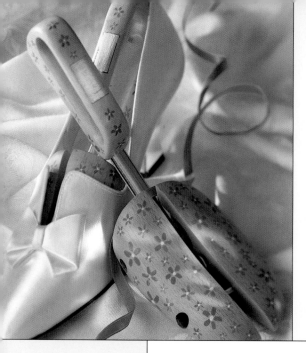

# DECORATED SHOETREES

## YOU WILL NEED

► Pair wooden shoetrees
► Fine sandpaper
► Damp cloth
► Three complementary colors of craft, acrylic, or poster paints
► Palette/plate
► Artist's paintbrush
► Masking tape
► Gold or silver metallic paint
► Black acrylic paint
► Newspaper
► Satin varnish
► Paintbrush, to use with varnish

Give the shoetrees a light sanding to provide a suitable surface for the paint to adhere to. Wipe away any dust with a damp cloth.

Pour a little of each of your paints onto a palette or plate. Beginning at the tip of the shoetrees and working back, paint forget-me-nots. You can paint them freehand or trace the templates on page 118. Allow to dry.

To personalize your shoetrees, mask a small rectangle on the top of each and paint over in gold or silver paint. If your shoetrees have a label printed on them, use this area. When dry, paint the date of your wedding or your married name in the rectangle using the black paint. Allow to dry then carefully peel off the masking tape.

Lay the decorated shoetrees on the newspaper and give them one to two coats of clear varnish. Allow to dry overnight before use.

flowers

# CALLA LILY SHEAF

## YOU WILL NEED

- ▶ Eleven long-stemmed calla lilies
- ▶ Fifty stems of long bear grass
- ▶ Scissors
- ▶ 3 feet of narrow cream ribbon
- ▶ Ruler
- ▶ Large sharp knife
- ▶ 2 feet of cream satin ribbon, 1-inch wide

◀ Lay the lilies on a work surface facing up. Divide the grass into five piles. Lay the lily with the longest stem on a clear part of the work surface. Lay a lily on either side of it 1 or 2 inches lower than the tip of the main flower. Arrange the remaining lilies and grass piles around these three flowers setting each flower head at a different height to its neighbor. Position the grass piles so that each extends beyond the main flowers. The bouquet should look long and graceful, not symmetrical and over-arranged.

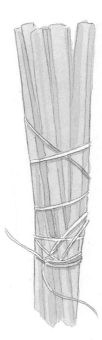

▲ Ease the narrow ribbon behind the stems and wrap it around the bundle of flowers. Tie a knot about halfway down the stems. Measure about 2 feet from the base of the bottom flower and trim the stems level using a sharp knife.

▲ Wrap the ribbon down the length of the stems crisscrossing the ribbon at the front. Tie a double knot at the back of the bouquet and trim away any surplus ribbon.

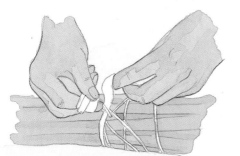

◀ Thread the wide ribbon under the narrow ribbon at the top of the binding and tie a large decorative bow. Trim a diagonal at each ribbon end.

# RED ROSES AND BERRY BOUQUET

## YOU WILL NEED

- ► Ten open, deep red roses
- ► Scissors
- ► Ten 1-foot lengths of medium-gauge florist's wire
- ► Florist's tape
- ► Bunch of large ivy leaves
- ► Ten sprigs of hypericum berries
- ► Ten large clumps of ivy berries and leaves
- ► Ten sprigs of box
- ► 10 redcurrant stems
- ► Ten 6-inch lengths of fine-gauge florist's wire
- ► Masking tape
- ► 2 feet cream satin ribbon, 1-inch wide

▲ Trim the stems of the roses so that only 1 inch of stem is left beneath each calyx. Using a length of medium-gauge wire, carefully push it up through the stem and calyx of each flower. Wrap 2 inches of florist's tape around the stem and wire to secure them.

► Trim the stems of all the components, except the redcurrants, to 3 inches in length. Because the redcurrants have such delicate stems they will need to be wired. Bend a 2-inch loop at the end of one of the lengths of fine-gauge wire, place this loop just beneath the fruit, then twist the loop around the stem and around the other end of the wire to secure. Repeat with remaining redcurrant stems.

◄ Divide the ivy leaves, hypericum sprigs, ivy clumps, and box sprigs equally into 10 groups. Arrange the stems of each group around a rose then bind the wires and stems together with about 3 inches of florist's tape. Repeat to make 10 small arrangements. Set the arrangements containing the longest pieces of trailing ivy to one side.

Pick the best small arrangement (one with no trailing ivy) and lay the wired stalks across the palm of your left hand, flowers facing away from you. Start adding the other groups of flowers one by one, binding the wired stems together with florist's tape. Keep adding the groups of flowers so you end up with an oval arrangement with trailing ivy at its base. Continue binding with tape to within about 4 inches of the ends of the wires.

▼ Bind the ends of the wires together with masking tape to finish and secure. Start wrapping the bound stems with ribbon, wrapping it closely to obscure the wires and tape. Cover to the base of the handle and then wrap back on itself and secure with a bow just beneath the bouquet.

### YOU WILL NEED

- ► Fourteen cornflowers
- ► Seven 3-inch lengths of delphinium flowers
- ► Seven 8-inch sprigs of variegated ivy
- ► Fourteen sprigs of lady's mantle
- ► Fourteen white- and purple-edged lizianthus
- ► Fourteen 6-inch and four 1-foot lengths of fine-gauge florist's wire
- ► Seven 1-foot lengths of medium-gauge florist's wire
- ► Scissors
- ► Florist's tape
- ► Four large ivy leaves
- ► Masking tape
- ► 2 feet of cream satin ribbon, 1-inch wide

COUNTRY

# SUMMER FLOWER BOUQUET

Cut the stems of all the bouquet components (except the ivy sprigs and delphiniums) to about 3 inches in length.

▲ Bend a 2-inch loop at the end of a 6-inch length of fine-gauge wire, lay this loop along the stem just beneath the flowers on a sprig of lady's mantle, then wrap the wire loop around the stem and around the other end of the wire. Wire the remaining lady's mantle in the same way.

► Divide the components of the bouquet into seven groups, with two cornflowers, lady's mantle, and lizianthus flowers in each group. Hold a length of medium-gauge wire along the stem of the delphinium starting about 1 inch beneath the bottom flowers, and bind wire and stem together with a little florist's tape. Arrange the other components around the delphinium flowers and bind to the wire. Repeat to make seven groups of flowers and foliage.

◄ Cut the stalks of the large ivy leaves to about 4 inches in length. Take a 1-foot length of fine-gauge wire and push it through the leaf from the back to the front, close to the central vein and about one-third of the way up the leaf. Push the wire back through the leaf on the other side of the vein and then twist the two ends of wire down the stalk. Repeat with the remaining leaves.

► Place three of the flower groups together and bind the stems and wires with tape. As you wrap down the length of the wires introduce the other wired groups, positioning the flowers slightly outward and a little lower than the first group of flowers. Continue taping and adding flowers until you have a well-shaped circle of blooms with a slightly domed appearance if viewed from the side. Position the ivy leaves just beneath the flowers, overlapping them slightly and taping in place. Continue taping the remainder of the wires so that you have a handle measuring about 5 to 6 inches in length. Trim any surplus wire away and wrap the base of the handle with a little masking tape. Wrap to the base of the bound stems with ribbon, then wrap the ribbon back on itself and tie with a bow at the top of the handle.

## YOU WILL NEED

► Twenty 1-foot and five 6-inch lengths of medium-gauge florist's wire
► Eight small double orange gerbera
► Florist's tape
► Five lime green chrysanthemums
► Seven large yellow thistles
► Scissors
► Seven stems of hypericum berries
► Five bright pink peonies
► Five large stems of umbrella plant
► Eight large green ivy leaves
► Eight 1-foot lengths of fine-gauge florist's wire
► 2 feet of cream satin ribbon, 1-inch wide

MODERN
# FUNKY POSY

◀ Take a 1-foot length of medium-gauge wire. Thread 2 inches of the length of wire through the widest part of the calyx of one gerbera, twist the ends of the wire together beneath the calyx and then wrap a little florist's tape around the calyx and twisted wires to secure. As you wrap the tape pull it taut and stretch it slightly. Repeat with the remaining chrysanthemums and gerberas.

▶ Trim the stems of the thistles so that only 1 inch of stem is left beneath each flower. Thread a 1-foot length of medium-gauge wire through the stem of a thistle just beneath the base of the flower. Push the wire through the stem so that about 2 inches protrudes from the other side then twist this down and around the other end of the wire. Trim the stems of hypericum so that the stem beneath the berries measures about 2 inches. Lay the stem alongside the thistle and wrap 2 inches of florist's tape around the wires and stalks to secure the two together, pulling and stretching the tape as you wrap. Repeat with the remaining thistles and hypericum.

◀ Trim the stems of the peonies so that 3 inches of stem is left beneath each flower. Cut the umbrella plant so that the stalk beneath the lower leaves measures about 3 inches. Lay a 6-inch length of medium wire alongside the stem of the peony so that the end of the wire is about 1 inch from the base of the flower, and tape wire and stem together with florist's tape until secure. Lay the umbrella plants alongside the taped peony and wire, tape the two together with about 2 inches of florist's tape. Repeat with the remaining peony and umbrella plant stems.

▶ Cut the stalks of the ivy leaves to about 4 inches in length and wire using a 1-foot length of fine-gauge florist's wire. Do this in exactly the same way as described on page 29.

▼ Pick the best of each of your wired blooms (not the ivy leaves) and hold them in your left hand. Position them so that they sit together neatly, and then bind the wired stems together with florist's tape. As you wrap down the length of the wires introduce the other wired blooms, positioning the second row of blooms slightly lower than the first, placing different colored flowers beside each other. Continue taping and adding flowers until you have a well-shaped bouquet. Position the ivy leaves just beneath the flowers, overlapping the leaves slightly and taping in place. Continue taping the remainder of the wires so you have a handle measuring about 5 to 6 inches in length. Trim any surplus wire away and bind the base of the handle in tape. Cover to the base of the bound stems with ribbon, binding closely to obscure the wires and tape. Wrap the ribbon back on itself and secure with a bow at the top of the handle.

## YOU WILL NEED

(All quantities depend on size of basket)

- ► Woven wicker or twig basket
- ► Scissors
- ► Lightweight fabric to line the inside of the basket
- ► Hot-melt glue gun
- ► Narrow yellow ribbon, 1½ times the length of the basket handle
- ► Modeling material, in two complementary colors
- ► Rolling pin
- ► Five-petal flower cutter, 2 inches in diameter
- ► Small sharp knife
- ► Cookie sheet
- ► Small paintbrush
- ► Cooling rack

# FLOWER GIRL'S BASKET

▲ Check over the basket and trim off any stray ends. Lay the lining material inside the basket easing around the edges and the base, and laying the surplus over the edge. Trim the fabric to within 1 inch of the top edge of the basket. Fold the excess fabric to the inside to give a nice neat edge and glue to the wicker using the glue gun. Continue until the whole piece has been glued securely in place. If you don't have a glue gun, the fabric can be loosely sewn to the inside of the basket with long, straight stitches in coordinating thread.

On a clean surface, thinly roll a little of the modeling material to about $\frac{1}{16}$ inch thick and stamp out flower shapes. Score a line down the center of each petal using the knife then stick the flowers together in pairs with a little water. Reroll the modeling material and repeat until you have enough flowers to go around the edge of the basket.

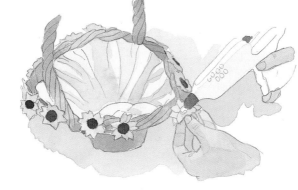

▶ Roll the second modeling material into tiny balls and fix 10 to 12 in a circle in the center of each flower. Arrange flowers on a cookie sheet and preheat the oven according to modeling materials instructions; bake for the required length of time. Allow to cool for 10 minutes then lift onto a cooling rack to cool completely.

▼ Spread glue on the back of each flower, leave for a few minutes, and when the glue is tacky, fix the flowers around the basket edge. Because the wicker and twig are not absorbent, be sure to use plenty of glue to fix the flowers firmly in place.

▶ Glue one end of the ribbon to the inside of one end of the handle. Wrap the ribbon around the handle following the design in the weave, glue in place at the other end, and trim away surplus ribbon.

## YOU WILL NEED

- ▶ Paper and scissors
- ▶ Pins
- ▶ 12 inches of pink dupion silk, 45-inches wide
- ▶ 12-inches of heavy-weight stiffener, 45-inches wide
- ▶ Iron
- ▶ Pale pink cotton thread
- ▶ Sewing machine
- ▶ Ruler and pencil
- ▶ Twenty pearl beads
- ▶ Needle
- ▶ Medium-gauge florist's wire
- ▶ Florist's tape
- ▶ Ten to twelve large pale pink roses
- ▶ Ten to twelve sprigs of lady's mantle
- ▶ Serrated knife
- ▶ Floral foam

# FLOWER-FILLED BRIDESMAID'S BAG

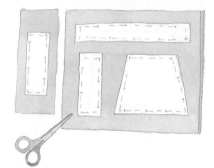

▲ Trace the patterns on page 119 onto paper. Cut out pattern pieces for two side panels, two end panels, one base, and two handles. Pin the paper pattern to the silk so that the grain runs horizontally across the side panels. Cut out the pieces. Cut out a second set of pieces from the stiffener and iron these to the back of the corresponding pieces of fabric.

► Lay one end piece on the base, good sides together. Using the pink cotton, sew together at one end leaving a ½-inch seam allowance. Sew the second end piece to the other end of the base. Trim away excess fabric from the seams. Pin this long strip around the three short edges of one of the side panels. Baste and then stitch in place leaving a ½-inch seam. Trim away excess fabric and clip corners. Repeat with the remaining side panel. Turn the bag right-side out. Turn over a ½-inch

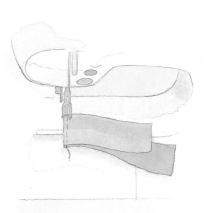

hem along the top edge of the bag, baste, and then top-stitch in place. Fold the handle pieces lengthwise twice so they are 1-inch wide and the raw edge is on the underside. Top-stitch down the center of each handle then stitch to the bag on the inside.

◄ Lay the bag flat and, using a ruler, make a small pencil mark where each bead is to be sewn in place. Double thread the needle with pink cotton and stitch beads to the bag, securing with small knots on the reverse side.

▼ Cut 10, 4-inch lengths of florist's wire. Trim the stems of the roses to the base of the calyx and push a wire up through the calyx of each rose. Tape a sprig of lady's mantle to the wired stem of each rose. Using a serrated knife, pare the floral foam down so that it sits snugly inside the bag and the bag has a nice shape. Arrange the roses in the foam so that they cover it completely. Make as close to the time of the wedding as possible so that the flowers remain in good condition.

## YOU WILL NEED

- ► Scissors
- ► Ten large half-open pale pink roses
- ► Ten large half-open cream roses
- ► Ten large half-open yellow roses
- ► Thirty 1-foot lengths of medium-gauge florist's wire
- ► Florist's tape
- ► Six to eight large green leaves, such as galax or ivy, with long stalks
- ► Four 1-foot lengths of fine-gauge florist's wire
- ► Masking tape
- ► 2 feet of cream satin ribbon, 1-inch wide

# BRIDESMAID'S ROSE ORB

► Trim the stems of the roses to the base of the calyx and thread a 1-foot length of medium-gauge wire up through the calyx of each rose. Bind the calyx and top of the wire with tape to strengthen and finish.

► Divide the roses into three groups, a cross-section of the three colors in each. Leave the wires of one group straight, bend the wires of the second group to about 45 degrees and then bend a 60-degree angle in the wires of the third group. Bend the wire just beneath the calyx.

Cut the stalks of the galax or ivy leaves to about 4 inches in length. Cut four 1-foot lengths of the fine florist's wire. Take a length of wire and push it through the leaf from the back to the front, close to the central vein and about one-third of the way up the leaf. Push the wire back through the leaf on the other side of the vein and then twist the two ends of wire down the stalk. Repeat with remaining leaves.

► Lay the straight wires of a white, pink, and cream rose across the palm of your left hand, roses facing away from you. Bind the wires together with a little tape. Start adding to the bouquet the roses with straight stems first and then use the bent ones around the edge of the bouquet to create the ball effect. Be sure to position different colored roses beside each other.

► Position the galax or ivy leaves just beneath the flowers, overlap the leaves slightly and tape in place. Trim the handle to about 6 inches in length and wrap the base of the handle with a little masking tape. Start wrapping the bound stems with ribbon, wrapping it closely to obscure the wires and tape. Wrap to the base of the handle then wrap the ribbon back on itself and secure with a bow at the top of the handle.

# RIBBON AND ROSE BOW

## YOU WILL NEED

(For each pew end)

- ▶ 6 feet of colored paper ribbon
- ▶ Scissors
- ▶ Ruler
- ▶ Stapler
- ▶ Three white roses
- ▶ Few sprigs of green foliage
- ▶ Raffia
- ▶ 2 feet of cream satin ribbon, 1-inch wide

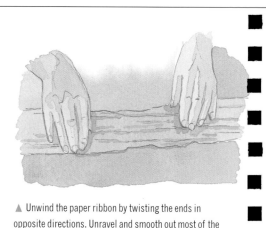

▲ Unwind the paper ribbon by twisting the ends in opposite directions. Unravel and smooth out most of the large creases. Cut off a 5-inch piece and set aside.

► Measure 10 inches in from one end of the longer piece of paper ribbon, you will start making loops from here. Make a loop using about 10 inches of ribbon then make a second loop a little larger, and then two further loops about the same size as the first two. Staple through the center of the loopy bow to secure. Wrap the reserved paper ribbon around the center of the bow and secure with staples.

► Trim the stems of the roses to 3 inches in length, arrange a little foliage around them and tie in a bunch with a short length of raffia.

► Lay the flowers in the middle of the satin ribbon so that there are equal amounts of ribbon on either side. Wrap the ribbon down and back up the stems of the roses, crisscrossing it neatly, and then secure with a bow beneath the blooms. Trim the ends of all the ribbons to finish, and then staple the back of the satin bow to the front of the paper bow, hiding the staple where it cannot be seen. Thread a length of raffia through the back of the bow and use to tie to the pew.

ROMANTIC

# GOLDEN WINTER CONES

## YOU WILL NEED

(For each pew end)

- ► Seven assorted clean, dry pine cones
- ► Newspaper
- ► Gold spray paint
- ► Scissors
- ► 3 feet of cream ribbon, ¼-inch wide
- ► Hot-melt glue gun or all-purpose glue
- ► 1½ feet of red and gold wired ribbon, 2-inches wide
- ► Embossing foil
- ► Pencil

► In a well ventilated room or outside, spread the pine cones on the newspaper and lightly spray with the paint. Allow to dry.

◄ Cut the cream ribbon into seven slightly different lengths and glue a length to the base of each cone.

▲ Tie the red ribbon in a bow and secure at the back with a little glue. Group the cream ribbons together, thread through the back of the ribbon bow, and tie with a knot. Tie a small loop in the end of one of the ribbons so the decoration can be hung up, and then trim the ends.

▲ ◄ Cut out a heart-, diamond-, or other shaped piece of foil. Lay on the newspaper and emboss a design around the edge using the pencil and applying even pressure. Glue the shape in the center of the bow and allow to dry.

COUNTRY

# APPLE WREATH

### YOU WILL NEED

(For each pew end)

- ► Two red apples
- ► 2 tablespoons of table salt
- ► 2 tablespoons of lemon juice
- ► 1 pint of cold water
- ► Paper towels
- ► Cooling rack
- ► All-purpose glue
- ► Straw wreath about 8 inches in diameter
- ► Sixteen ears of dyed dried wheat
- ► Raffia
- ► Fine wire
- ► 2 feet of wired peach ribbon, 2-inches wide

► Slice the apples into thin rings.
Put the salt and lemon juice in a bowl and stir in 1 pint cold water.
Add the apple slices, put a plate on top of them to prevent them from floating, and allow to stand for 10 minutes. Drain well and pat dry with paper towels. Spread the apple slices on a cooling rack and bake at 140°F for 2 to 4 hours. After 2 hours check the apples for dryness and continue to cook if necessary. The slices are dry when they have a leathery feel and are still pliable. Remove from the oven and allow to cool completely.

▶ Lightly spread the back of each apple slice with glue and arrange in an overlapping circle around the front of the wreath. Leave to dry.

▲ Divide the wheat into two piles, arrange each pile in a fan shape, and tie the stalks tightly with raffia. Trim the stalks to within 1 inch of the ears.

◀ Cut a 1-foot length of fine wire and use it to bind the two bunches of wheat to the bottom of the raffia wreath, stalks facing inward, crossing where tied with raffia and ears of wheat facing out. Cut a 1-foot piece of ribbon, fold in half, and tuck the loop through the wreath. Push the cut ends through the loop and pull tightly. Tie the remaining ribbon in a bow and glue to the front of the wreath where the wheat stalks cross.

# GRASS AND GLORY LILY CIRCLE

## YOU WILL NEED

- ► Floral foam-filled plastic pew end decoration
- ► 1½ feet of coordinating ribbon, ½-inch wide
- ► Scissors and ruler
- ► Five 6-inch lengths of equisetum
- ► Mixed foliage such as umbrella plant, hebe stems, and galax leaves
- ► Small bunch of bear grass
- ► Four 3-inch lengths of medium-gauge florist's wire
- ► Florist's tape
- ► 5 *Gloriosa* (glory lilies)

Soak the plastic pew end decoration in a bowl of cold water until it sinks. This indicates that it is full of water. Tie the ribbon to the back. Leave the ends long so that it can be tied in place and the surplus ribbon trimmed away when assembled in position.

▲ Trim the equisetum down to 5-inch lengths, cutting a diagonal at each end. Cut the stems of the galax down to 2 inches in length, and the hebe and umbrella plants into small branches measuring from 3 to 5 inches.

▲ Hold the grass in a bunch and trim the ends so that the bunch measures about 10 inches. Divide the grass into four and cut four 3-inch lengths of wire. Take one of the bunches of grass and fold in half. Push a wire inside the bunch so that only 1 inch of wire is showing. Tightly wrap the grass and wire with florist's tape. Repeat to make four bunches.

▼ Start arranging the components of the decoration in the foam keeping the large flat galax leaves toward the edges to give shape and width to the decoration and spreading the other materials evenly around the arrangement. Complete by trimming the stems of the glory lilies and distributing them evenly among the foliage. Mist with cold water and store in a cool place until ready to use.

# CONFETTI

## TULLE PURSES

### FOR EACH PURSE YOU WILL NEED

- ▶ 10-inch square of nylon tulle
- ▶ Scissors
- ▶ Small handful of petal-shaped paper confetti or dried rose-petal confetti
- ▶ Two 8-inch lengths of coordinating ribbon, 1½-inches wide

Fold the square of tulle lengthwise in half and half again to form a narrow strip. Cut a serrated edge along each narrow end and then open out the tulle. Place some confetti along one straight side. Carefully roll the tulle over the confetti and continue rolling until you have a tube shape. Tie at each end with a ribbon bow.

## VIOLET AND PANSY CORNETS

### FOR EACH CORNET YOU WILL NEED

- ▶ 10-inch fancy white doily
- ▶ Double-sided sticky tape
- ▶ 10 inches of coordinating ribbon, ½-inch wide
- ▶ Scissors
- ▶ Fresh or dried violets and/or pansies

Fold the doily in half and roll into a cornet shape securing with a strip of double-sided tape. Fold the ribbon in half and mark the center. Lay the join of the cornet on the center of the ribbon and draw the ribbon ends round to the front of the cornet. Cross them over each other and secure with a small piece of double-sided tape. Trim the ends to neaten and then fill the cornet with fresh or dried violets and/or pansies. (To dry violets and pansies seal the flowers in a large paper bag. Leave in a dark warm place for several weeks after which time the petals will be shrunken and dried. Keep there until ready to use or in a sealed cardboard box with a light sprinkling of silica gel. The silica gel will keep the petals dry and absorb any moisture.)

## FERTILITY CONFETTI

### FOR EACH BOX YOU WILL NEED

- ► 6-inch sheet of thin white cardboard
  or heavy paper
- ► Scissors
- ► Craft knife
- ► Glue or double-sided sticky tape
- ► Ten ears of dried wheat
- ► 8 inches of decorative paper,
  1½-inches wide
- ► Raffia

Trace the box template on page 119 onto the back of the cardboard or paper. Cut out using the scissors then, using the knife, score along the fold lines. Glue the tab in place and bend in the flaps to give the box a concave shape at each end. Run your hands down the length of eight ears of wheat to pull off the seeds. Fill the box with wheat, wrap with the decorative paper, and seal at the back with a dot of glue or a piece of tape. Tie the box with raffia and then decorate with remaining ears of wheat.

## CHERUB PAPER POCKETS

### FOR EACH BOX YOU WILL NEED

- ► 6-inch sheet of medium-weight
  decorative paper
- ► Cherub rubber stamp
- ► Lilac-colored ink pad
- ► Scissors
- ► Craft knife
- ► Glue or double-sided sticky tape
- ► Confetti of your choice
- ► 1 foot of decorative ribbon,
  ½-inch wide

Trace the box template on page 119 onto the back of the paper. Turn the paper good side up and stamp with cherubs. When dry, cut out using the scissors and then score along the fold lines using the knife. Glue the tab in place and then bend in the flaps to give the box a concave shape at each end. Fill with confetti and tie with a ribbon bow.

# BOUTONNIERES

## ORCHID

### YOU WILL NEED

► Two small, white orchids
► Scissors
► 2 inches of heavy-gauge florist's wire
► Florist's tape

Trim the stems of the orchids to 2 inches in length. Lay an orchid on either side of the wire and bind the stems and wire together using a couple of inches of florist's tape, wrapping the tape in a spiral down the length of the wire. Trim the ends to neaten, mist with cold water, and keep in a cool place until required.

## RED ROSE AND IVY

### YOU WILL NEED

► One medium-size open red rose
► Scissors
► 2 inches of heavy-gauge florist's wire
► Florist's tape
► Small sprig of winter berries
► Two small sprigs of large-leafed ivy

Trim the stem of the rose to just beneath the calyx. Carefully push the wire up through the calyx. Bind the calyx and wire with a couple of inches of florist's tape. Bind the sprig of berries to a 2-inch length of wire. Group together the rose, berries, and ivy, positioning the ivy around the rose. Bind the stems and wires with tape. Trim ends to neaten, mist with cold water, and keep in a cool place.

## FRAGRANT HERBS

### YOU WILL NEED

► Two chive or thrift flowers
► Two small sprigs of rosemary
► Two bay leaves
► One small sprig of variegated hebe
► Scissors
► 2 inches of heavy-gauge florist's wire
► Florist's tape
► 6 inches of narrow cream velvet ribbon

Trim the stems of all the flowers and leaves so that they measure between 4 and 5 inches in length. Arrange into a little bunch with the flowers at the front. Push the piece of wire inside the bunch of stems and then bind the top 1 inch of the stems, nearest the flowers, and wire with tape. Wrap all but the tip of the stems with ribbon and secure at the back with a little knot.

## STEPHANOTIS AND IVY CORSAGE

### YOU WILL NEED

- ▶ 4 inches of fine-gauge florist's wire
- ▶ 3-inch stem of stephanotis flowers
- ▶ Sprig of variegated ivy, 6-inches long
- ▶ 2 inches of heavy-gauge florist's wire
- ▶ Florist's tape
- ▶ Scissors

Bend the fine-gauge wire into a hairpin shape with one leg longer than the other. Hold the "u" shape against the stem of the stephanotis, just beneath the flowers, and wind the longer leg around the flower stem and shorter leg to support the flowerhead. Lay the sprig of ivy behind the stephanotis and the heavy wire between the two. Bind with a couple of inches of florist's tape, wrapping the tape in a spiral down the length of the stems and wire. Trim ends to neaten, mist with cold water, and keep in a cool place.

## COUNTRY CORSAGE

### YOU WILL NEED

- ▶ Three single delphinium flowers with stalks
- ▶ 4 inches of fine-gauge florist's wire
- ▶ Two sprigs of cow parsley
- ▶ Sprig of variegated hebe
- ▶ Florist's tape
- ▶ Scissors

Hold the delphiniums in a group. Bend the fine-gauge wire into a hairpin shape with one leg longer than the other. Hold the "u" shape against the stems, just beneath the flowers, and wind the longer leg around the flower stems and shorter leg, to keep the corsage from drooping. Group together the cow parsley and hebe, and arrange the delphiniums at the front. Push the piece of wire inside the bunch of stems and then bind with florist's tape, wrapping the tape in a spiral down the length of the stems and wire. Trim ends to neaten, mist with cold water, and keep in a cool place until required.

## RUBEKIA

### YOU WILL NEED

- ► One rubekia flower or large yellow daisy
- ► Scissors
- ► Two 2-inch lengths of heavy-gauge florist's wire
- ► Few sprigs golden rod
- ► Florist's tape
- ► 8 inches of ½ inch wide white velvet ribbon
- ► Long pin

Trim the stems of the rubekia to 2 inches in length. Carefully push a piece of wire up the stem. Arrange the rubekia and golden rod and then wrap the stems with a couple of inches of florist's tape. Wrap the stems with the ribbon spiraling it down and then up, securing it at the back with a pin. Carefully bend the rubekia so that the flower faces forward. Mist with water and keep cool until required.

## FLOWER GALLERY

Many different flowers can be used to make beautiful boutonnieres. Here are a few ideas for other flowers that you might like to use.

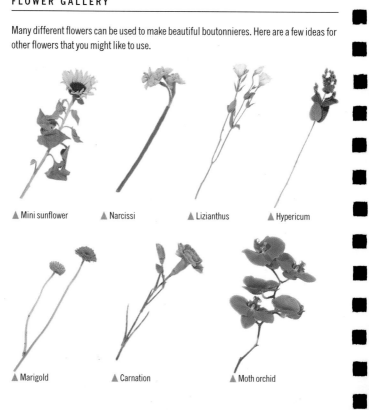

▲ Mini sunflower      ▲ Narcissi      ▲ Lizianthus      ▲ Hypericum

▲ Marigold      ▲ Carnation      ▲ Moth orchid

stationery

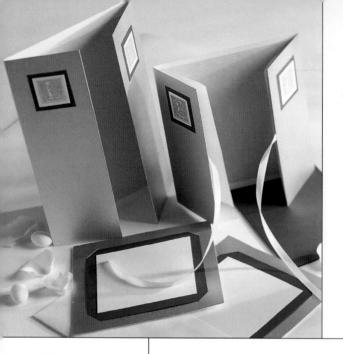

## YOU WILL NEED

- ► Pencil
- ► Thin silver cardboard
- ► Scissors
- ► Craft knife
- ► Cutting mat
- ► Ruler
- ► Textured pale blue paper
- ► Paper glue
- ► 6½-inch square dark blue or silver-colored envelopes, one for each invitation
- ► Thin dark blue cardboard
- ► Initial stamps
- ► Embossing ink
- ► Silver embossing powder
- ► Heat gun
- ► Thin white cardboard
- ► 1 foot of narrow white ribbon per invitation

WEDDING INVITATIONS: TRADITIONAL

# THREE-FOLD
# SILVER

▲ For the invitation trace the template on page 120 onto the silver cardboard and cut out. Score the fold lines and fold inward to make the flaps. Repeat with the pale blue paper (your text should be printed or stuck onto this paper). Glue a paper insert inside each invitation. Check that the invitations fit the envelopes you have. The order of ceremony and menu cards are made in the same way. As they don't require an envelope they can be made as large or small as you like, and you can omit the paper liner.

▶◀ Trace the template on page 120 that is to be used for the decorative panel on blue cardboard. Print initials within the squares onto the blue cardboard (you will need two for every item of stationery you wish to decorate). Sprinkle each print with a little silver embossing powder, tap away the excess, then heat the powder gently with the heat gun. As it gets hot it will melt to give a raised silver design. Be careful not to hold the heat source too close to the cardboard or it may burn.

▼ Trace the template from page 120 for the decorative panel on white cardboard. Cut out. Glue a blue square to the front of every white square and glue one of each initial to the front of every item of stationery, except the evening invitations. Cut two 6-inch lengths of ribbon and glue a piece to the inside edge of each invitation. When dry, fold the cards closed and tie the ribbon in a bow.

Cut out the evening invitation cards following the template on page 120. Cut the slot marks using a craft knife. The smallest square of the template is the area for your text. Glue your text to the blue squares then push the corners of the blue squares through the slots in the silver cardboard. The back of the invitation can be used to show a map or details of hotels.

## YOU WILL NEED

- ► Thin cream cardboard
- ► Heavily textured gold paper
- ► Scissors
- ► Craft knife
- ► Ruler
- ► Paper glue
- ► 11¾ x 8¼-inch envelopes, one for every invitation
- ► Thin red cardboard
- ► Thick fancy red paper
- ► Entwined hearts stamp
- ► Embossing ink
- ► Gold embossing powder
- ► Heat gun

ROMANTIC

# HEARTS OF GOLD

▲ For each invitation and menu trace the templates on page 121 onto cream cardboard and gold paper. Cut out. Score the fold lines on the cream cardboard with a craft knife, fold in half, and paste the gold paper to the front. Check that the invitations fit the envelopes.

▶ Following the templates on page 121, cut out one cream and one red panel for each invitation and menu card. Print a heart on the top of each cream panel, sprinkle each print with a little gold embossing powder, tap away the excess, and then heat the powder gently with the heat gun. As it gets hot it will melt to give a raised design. Be careful not to hold the heat source too close to the cardboard otherwise you may burn it. Glue the cream and red cards together in pairs and glue one to the front of each invitation or menu.

◀ Cut out the name cards in red and cream following the template on page 121. Emboss hearts on the cream cardboard and then paste the cream cardboard onto the red (as above). Score and cut as per template. Fold the cards in half so that the heart shapes protrude above the fold and stand out in relief.

◀ Cut out and score the evening reception envelopes and card following the template on page 121. Cut out the gold and cream inserts and paste one on top of the other. Glue a pair of cards to the inside of each envelope. The cream cards can be printed with the wedding text or the text can be printed to size and pasted to them. The smaller RSVP cards and envelopes are made following the templates on page 121. Make the envelopes in gold textured paper and the cards from red cardboard decorated with a cream embossed panel.

## YOU WILL NEED

- ► Small fresh flowers
- ► Flower press, or blotting paper and heavy books
- ► Thin metallic silver cardboard
- ► Scissors
- ► Craft knife
- ► Ruler
- ► Selection of different colored/textured papers and tissues
- ► Pretty 6 x 8¼-inch envelopes, one for each invitation
- ► Paper glue
- ► Artist's paintbrush
- ► Small feathers
- ► Hole puncher
- ► Small raffia bows

COUNTRY

# PRESSED PETALS PAPER

◀ Pick a selection of small fresh, unblemished flowers. Trim the stalks and arrange the flowers facing downward on the pages of the flower press. Assemble the press and leave the flowers to dry for about 2 to 3 weeks. If you don't have a press, arrange the flowers on sheets of blotting paper. Cover each sheet with a second sheet of paper and sandwich these between the pages of heavy hardback books.

▶ Trace the template on page 122 for the invitation and order of ceremony onto the silver cardboard. Cut out. Score down the center using a craft knife. Fold in half and then check they fit inside the envelopes.

◀ Tear a large rectangle of decorative paper and glue to the front of each card (see template on page 122). To tear a straight line, lay a ruler on the paper and carefully tear the paper against the edge of the ruler, using it as a guide. In the same way, tear two or three more small, differently colored and textured rectangles of paper. Glue the papers to the front of the cards overlapping the pieces slightly. Using a small paintbrush, spread a little glue on the back of the dried flowers, feathers, and raffia bows. Glue a selection to the front of each card.

◀ Cut out name labels on decorative paper using the template on page 122. Punch a hole in the corner of each label and thread with raffia. Glue a small colored paper rectangle to each label, add a dried flower, write a name in italic script, and allow to dry.

## MODERN
# DAISY PYRAMIDS

### YOU WILL NEED

- ▶ White 140 lb watercolor paper
- ▶ Craft knife
- ▶ Ruler
- ▶ 6½-inch square colored envelopes, one for each invitation
- ▶ Masking fluid
- ▶ Artist's paintbrush
- ▶ Lilac, yellow, and green watercolor paint
- ▶ Scissors
- ▶ Paper glue
- ▶ Fine tip black ink-pen

▲ Trace the templates on page 123 and transfer the shape of the item you wish to make onto a sheet of watercolor paper. Cut out using a craft knife and score along the fold lines, being careful not to cut through the paper. Check that the invitations fit into the envelopes.

▶ Trace the triangle and daisy template, for the item you are making, from page 123, and transfer to a sheet of watercolor paper. Tip a little masking fluid into a small container and paint the head of the daisy within the triangle.

▶ When dry, apply a thin wash of lilac paint over the entire triangle and leave to dry. Rub your fingertip across the dried masking fluid, which will roll into balls revealing white paper beneath. Paint in the center of the daisy and the stalk, and then cut out the triangles, cutting slightly inside the marked lines.

◀ Glue the triangles to the invitations, menus, and place cards. Write the wording onto the cards (the wording is included on the the templates on page 123 for your reference).

# SILVER DOVE PACKAGE

### YOU WILL NEED

- ► Cardboard gift box
- ► Brown paper (need sheet large enough to cover chosen box)
- ► Ruler and craft knife
- ► Paper glue
- ► Tape
- ► Dove stamp
- ► Embossing ink
- ► Silver embossing powder
- ► Heat gun
- ► Silver ribbon

▲ Stand the box on the brown paper. Make two cuts at right angles from each corner of the box one and a half times as long as the box is deep. Spread a little glue on the outside of the box and then fold the paper up the sides of the box. Turn the excess paper to the inside of the box, and secure with small pieces of tape. Repeat with the lid.

► Using the stamp and embossing ink, stamp several doves on one side of the box.

► Sprinkle the doves with embossing powder and then tip the box upright and tap lightly so that the excess dust falls away.

▼ Turn on the heat gun and when it reaches temperature hold it over each stamp and the heat will melt the dust to give an attractive silver embossed dove. Repeat with the remaining doves. Stamp the whole box and lid, and emboss as above. Tie with a ribbon bow and add a decorative stamped gift label.

## ROMANTIC
# PARTY FAVOR

### YOU WILL NEED
► Party favor kit
► Glue stick
► Sheet of giftwrap
► Cutting mat or old newspapers
► Craft knife
► Coordinating ribbon
► Coordinating card
► Scissors
► Heart stamp
► Coordinating ink

Prepare the party favor so that the cardboard is ready to fold as per instructions. Lightly cover with adhesive and then lay face down on the back of the sheet of giftwrap.

◄ Press the cardboard down firmly, turn over, and smooth out any small creases in the paper. Lay on the cutting mat and cut away the excess paper from around the favor using a craft knife. Carefully cut out any areas that are not required and then fold the box along its pre-scored lines.

Tuck a gift inside the box and then finish assembling the favor. Tie a piece of ribbon around each end of the box in a bow. Cut out a label shape from the cardboard, print with a heart and a border in a coordinating ink. Glue to the front of the box when dry.

# POTPOURRI
# BOTTLE BAG

## YOU WILL NEED

- Coordinating patterned paper
- Scissors
- Paper bottle bag
- Clear-dry craft glue
- Four 1½-inch squares of burlap
- Five slices dried apple
- Six dried bay leaves
- Three pieces of whole star anise
- Raffia

Cut out a rectangle of paper a little smaller than the front of the bottle bag and glue it to the front of the bag.

▲ Lightly fray the edges of the burlap by pulling out and discarding two or three of the threads from each side. Layer up the burlap with the apple slices, bay leaves, and star anise, and glue to the front of the bag. Glue the remaining components into a little stack, thread with raffia, and tie to the handles of the bag.

STATIONERY

## MODERN
# ALL MY HEARTS DECORATED BAG

### YOU WILL NEED

- ► White or colored paper bag
- ► Ruler
- ► Pencil
- ► 6 brightly colored sheets of thick paper
- ► Scissors
- ► Paper glue
- ► Hole puncher
- ► Short length of narrow colored ribbon

◄ Press the bag flat, along pre-folded lines. Divide the width into three equal columns and the length into four equal columns. Mark lightly in pencil so that you have a grid. Cut out 12 equal squares or rectangles of colored paper, the dimensions should match the grid you have drawn. Glue the shapes neatly to the front of the bag. Cut out six small paper heart shapes (see template on page 123) and glue a heart to six of the squares.

Fold a small rectangle of colored paper in half to make a tag and decorate with four pieces of colored paper and two small heart shapes. Punch the upper left-hand corner of the card with a hole, thread with ribbon, and tie to the handle of the bag.

wedding table

## TABLE CENTERPIECE: TRADITIONAL
# ROSE-RING CANDLESTICK

### YOU WILL NEED

- ► Three white rosebuds
- ► Scissors
- ► Three 6-inch lengths of medium-gauge florist's wire
- ► Florist's tape
- ► Three 3-inch lengths of hypericum berries
- ► Nine 3-inch lengths of wax flowers
- ► Six 3-inch lengths of white chrysanthemum flower buds
- ► Four 3-inch lengths of eucalyptus
- ► Nine 3-inch lengths of lady's mantle
- ► Candlestick approximately 4 inches in diameter
- ► Pale blue candle

▲ Cut the stems from the roses to just beneath the calyxes. Thread a length of wire through the widest part of the calyx of one rose, twist the wires together beneath the calyx and wrap a little florist's tape around the calyx and twisted wires to secure. As you wrap, pull the tape taut and stretch it slightly. Repeat with the remaining rosebuds.

◀ Take a wired rosebud in your left hand, hold a little greenery beneath the rose and start wrapping the florist's tape down the wire of the rose, pulling the tape tightly and binding the greenery to the wire as you wrap. Continue wrapping in this way, adding lengths of hypericum berries, wax flowers, white chrysanthemum flower buds, eucalyptus, and lady's mantle. Use plenty of tape when wrapping and keep the roses and leaves of the greenery pointing in the same direction. Keep the garland lush and dense and continue until it is as long as the circumference of the candlestick base.

▼ Place the floral circlet around the base of the candlestick. Join the ends together and arrange the end to match the beginning. Secure with tape. Place the candle in the candlestick.

# ROSE AND LAVENDER BASKET

## YOU WILL NEED

- ► Tape measure
- ► Shallow wicker basket, approx 1 foot in diameter
- ► Double-sided tape
- ► Scissors
- ► Large bunch of fresh or dried lavender
- ► Raffia
- ► Large square of cellophane
- ► Four miniature red rose bushes
- ► Compost
- ► Dried moss

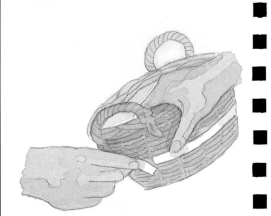

▲ Measure the circumference of the basket halfway between the base and rim. Cut a piece of tape 1 inch longer than this measurement. Remove the backing paper from one side and wrap the tape around the outside of the basket. Push the tape down well so that it adheres firmly.

▶ Measure the height of the basket. Divide the lavender into two batches. Trim the stems of one pile to the same height as the basket. Stick this batch around the outside of the basket keeping the stems to within ½ inch of each other.

▲ Double wrap the basket with raffia, positioning it over the tape. Tie in a knot and trim away any loose ends. Trim the stems of the remaining lavender so that it is slightly shorter than the height of the basket and then push individual sprigs between the lavender sprigs already wrapped around the basket to fill any gaps.

▶ Line the basket with the cellophane and then trim away any that protrudes over the edge. Remove the roses from the pots and stand in the basket. Fill in the gaps with tightly packed compost and then cover the surface of the soil with dried moss. Mist the flowers with water and keep the arrangement in a cool place until required.

## YOU WILL NEED

- ► Terra-cotta pot, the rim approximately 1-foot in diameter
- ► Newspaper or plastic bag
- ► Lilac latex paint
- ► Paintbrush
- ► Masking tape
- ► Four wooden skewers
- ► Large block of floral foam
- ► Bowl
- ► Large sheet of cellophane
- ► Craft knife
- ► Tall candle approx 3-inch diameter
- ► Scissors
- ► Assorted country flowers such as roses, scabious, and daisies
- ► Fine-gauge florist's wire
- ► Large ivy leaves

## COUNTRY
# FLORAL CANDLE POT

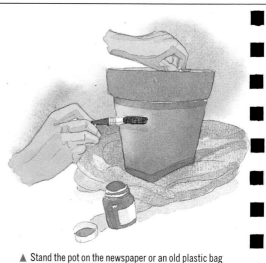

▲ Stand the pot on the newspaper or an old plastic bag and give the outside an even coat of latex paint. Let dry completely and then recoat if necessary.

► Tape four wooden skewers, making sure they are evenly spaced apart, around the bottom 1½ inches of the candle.

◄ Lay out sheets of newspaper. Using a sharp knife, cut the floral foam so that it fits snugly into the pot. Remove. Soak the foam in a bowl of cold water until it sinks. Fold the cellophane into quarters and use it to line the pot. Pack the pot with the wet foam and trim the top level. Push the candle into the foam and trim away the excess cellophane so that it is level with the top of the pot. Trim the foam around the candle base to give a neat dome shape.

▲ ▼ Trim the stems of the flowers and foliage to about 3 inches in length. Divide the flowers up into small sprays, each containing four to six stems of different flowers. Cut the florist's wire into 4-inch lengths and use it to bind each spray firmly together at the base. Arrange large ivy leaves around the base of the foam so that they overlap slightly and face up. Starting at the base and working up, push the sprays of flowers into the foam keeping the colors well mixed and the flowers evenly spaced. Continue pushing in sprays of flowers until the foam is completely hidden and the base of the candle covered. Never leave a lit candle unattended.

# GERBERA TREE

## YOU WILL NEED

- ► Tall slim terra-cotta pot, the rim approximately 7-inches in diameter
- ► Newspaper
- ► Lime-green latex paint
- ► Paintbrush
- ► Sharp knife
- ► Floral foam
- ► Large square of cellophane
- ► Scissors
- ► Nine to fifteen contrasting colored gerberas
- ► Fine-gauge florist's wire
- ► Enough dried moss to cover top of the pot

▲ Stand the pot on a sheet of newspaper and give the outside a coat of lime-green latex paint. When dry, recoat and then leave to dry completely. This will take about 15 minutes as terra-cotta is very absorbent and dries very quickly.

► Using the knife, pare down the floral foam so that it fits snugly inside the pot and finishes about 1 inch beneath the rim. The foam is very easy to cut but it makes lots of powdery dust so do this on a sheet of newspaper.

◄ Soak the foam in a bowl of water. Fold the cellophane into quarters and push it down into the pot, easing it around the base. Push the wet foam into the pot and then trim away any protruding cellophane.

▲ Arrange the gerberas in a ball shape with the heads facing out in all directions and the colors evenly distributed through the arrangement. Hold the stems just beneath the flower heads and securely wrap with 5 or 6 inches of florist's wire. Keep the wire as close to the flowers as possible so that it will be invisible when the decoration is complete. Decide how tall the finished table decoration is to be and trim the stems (they should be no shorter than 1 foot in length). Tie the stems together at the base with wire and then carefully push the bundle of stems into the foam, pushing them in as far as necessary to make the arrangement stable. Arrange the dried moss over the foam and then keep the arrangement in a cool place until required.

## TABLECLOTH AND NAPKIN: TRADITIONAL

# DESIGN IN RELIEF

### YOU WILL NEED

- ► White paper
- ► Thick black pen
- ► Tape
- ► Lightweight white fabric large enough to cover the top and sides of the table
- ► White puff dimensional fabric paint
- ► Colored napkins
- ► Clean cloth
- ► Iron
- ► Sewing machine
- ► White cotton thread
- ► Colored tablecloth

▲ Draw the design of your choice onto a sheet of white paper using a thick black pen; alternatively, enlarge and use the design on page 123. Tape the design to the table top and lay the fabric over the top; then tape the fabric to the table top or weight it down to hold it in place.

▲ Shake the paint container well, trim the tip off, and then trace the design by squeezing the paint and holding the nozzle just above the fabric. Take care not to smudge what you have just painted when untaping the fabric, repositioning it, and tracing the next section of the design. Continue all the way around the edge of the cloth then allow to dry for at least 4 hours. Repeat with the napkins using the same design, but smaller.

◀ Turn the tablecloth over so that it is good side down, cover the design with a clean cloth, and iron with a hot iron for 1 minute. The paint will puff up to produce an attractive raised design. Continue all the way round the edge of the cloth before pressing each of the napkins.

▶ If your tablecloth is made of fabric that will not fray, turn under and press a ½-inch hem all the way round the edge. Using the white thread, stitch in place with a long straight stitch. If your cloth is made of easily frayable or very lightweight sheer fabric you can give it an attractive frayed edging by pulling out the loose threads. Continue fraying the edges until they measure ¼ to ½ inch. Lay the colored cloth on the table. Lay the white cloth over the top so that the design hangs down the sides.

ROMANTIC

# ROSE AND IVY GARLAND

## YOU WILL NEED

► Iron
► Enough red velvet to cover top and sides of table
► Red cotton
► Sewing machine
► White cotton tablecloth
► Long branches of variegated ivy
► Paper towels
► Pins
► Small white, red, or orange fresh roses
► Scissors
► White napkins

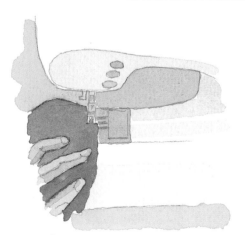

▲ Turn under and press ½-inch hem all the way round the edge of the red velvet. Using the red cotton, stitch in place with a long straight stitch.

Press the red cloth and lay on the table. Press the white cloth and lay it on top of the red one, so that it hangs in points between the corners of the red cloth.

▲ Wash the ivy thoroughly and pat dry with paper towels. Pick two equally long branches of ivy and carefully pin them to one corner of the white cloth. Pin from the back to the front and position the ivy so that the leaves face up. Secure with a pin every 4 or 5 inches.

▲ Sort through the roses and pick equally sized blooms; you will need approximately one rose per 1 foot of ivy garland. Trim the stems to just beneath the calyx. Pin the roses evenly along the length of the ivy garland, pinning from the back of the cloth and through the calyx. Turn the roses to face up and out. Secure any particularly large flowers with a second pin. Roll the napkins up and wrap each with a 6 to 7 inch length of clean ivy. Tuck a rose beneath each ring of ivy or lay a couple of roses with leaves on each dinner plate.

## YOU WILL NEED

- ► White cotton tablecloth or enough white cotton fabric to completely cover the table
- ► Yellow cotton gingham, long enough and wide enough to trim the white cloth with a 5-inch border
- ► Scissors
- ► Pins
- ► Pencil and ruler
- ► Sewing machine
- ► White thread
- ► Small daisy and leaf rubber stamps
- ► Yellow and green fabric paint
- ► Two saucers
- ► Iron

COUNTRY

# DAISIES AND GINGHAM

▼ Measure the length and width of the white cloth. Cut two strips of the gingham fabric each 5 inches wide and ½ inch longer than the length of the white cloth. Then cut two strips of the gingham fabric each 5 inches wide and ½ inch longer than the width of the white cloth

▼ Take one length-long and one width-long strip of gingham and lay them on top of each other with one set of raw ends matching. Pin the ends together. Measure

5 inches in from the top right-hand corner and draw a diagonal line to the bottom right hand corner. Pin in place and sew along this line. Trim away the small triangle of excess fabric from above the stitched line, and then press the seam open. Repeat with the remaining fabric to make four mitered corners. You will now have a large rectangular frame-shaped border.

▼ Clip the corners and turn a ½-inch hem around the inside edge of the border. Pin and press in place. Lay the tablecloth flat and pin the gingham border to the edge of the cloth matching the raw edges of the border with the raw edges of the cloth. Fold under a ½-inch hem, treating the double layer of fabric (gingham and tablecloth) as one. Pin in place. Stitch around the outside and inside edges of the gingham border. Trim away excess fabric and secure.

▼ Put a little of each paint color into separate saucers. Spread the tablecloth flat. Lightly dip the daisy stamp in the yellow paint and print flowers randomly around the edge of the cloth. Repeat with the leaf stamp, printing a leaf in between each flower. When dry, iron the cloth on the reverse to fix and set the paint.

## YOU WILL NEED

- ▶ Tracing paper and pencil
- ▶ Tape
- ▶ Stencil card
- ▶ Cutting mat
- ▶ Craft knife
- ▶ Enough pale blue cotton
  fabric to cover the top
  and sides of the table
- ▶ Pale blue thread
- ▶ Sewing machine
- ▶ Pins
- ▶ Ruler
- ▶ Re-positional adhesive
- ▶ White fabric paint
- ▶ Small dish
- ▶ Stencil brush
- ▶ Paper towel
- ▶ Iron
- ▶ Silver ribbon, ½-inch
  wide, enough to line the
  edge of the cloth
- ▶ Scissors
- ▶ White thread

MODERN

# CRAZY
# HEARTS

▲ Using the tracing paper and pencil trace the heart
design on page 124. Turn the tracing upside down and tape
it to the stencil card. Lightly rub over the designs with a
pencil to transfer the pencil lines to the card. Discard
tracing paper.

◄ Put the stencil card onto the cutting mat and using a craft knife carefully cut out the heart shapes. Take the blue fabric and turn under a ½-inch hem. Using the pale blue thread topstitch in place using a short straight stitch. Spread the tablecloth out flat on the work surface and position a line of pins, 1½ inches from the hem, along one edge. Apply re-positional adhesive to the reverse of the stencil and align the tip of the hearts with the pinned line.

► Tip a little white paint into a small dish. Dip the stencil brush into the paint, blot some of the paint onto a paper towel, and then stipple through the stencil. Carefully remove the stencil, reposition, and repeat all along one side of the cloth. Leave until touch dry before repeating along the remaining sides. Leave to dry as per manufacturer's instructions before ironing on the reverse to fix and set the fabric paint. Remove the line of pins.

◄ Pin the ribbon ¼-inch in from the edge of the cloth along one side. At the corner, fold the ribbon on the diagonal to turn the corner and continue pinning along the next side. Repeat along the remaining two sides, turning under the two raw ends to finish. Using white thread sew along the inside and outside edges of the ribbon using a straight stitch. Secure the ends and trim. To finish, press the border with the iron.

# PLACE SETTINGS

## MINIATURE CANDLE POTS

### YOU WILL NEED

► Small terra-cotta pots
► Paint
► Discs of cardboard or plastic
► Plaster of Paris
► Candles
► Dried moss
► Rubber stamp and ink
► Colored paper
► Corrugated cardboard
► Colored thread

Paint small terra-cotta pots in the color of your choice using acrylic, craft, or metallic spray paint. When dry, block the small hole in the base of each pot with a disc of cardboard or plastic, and then half-fill each pot with Plaster of Paris. Before the plaster sets, stand a small wax candle in the center. When dry, tuck dried moss around the top of the pot. Stamp names or initials onto colored paper, mount onto corrugated cardboard labels, and tie to the candle pots with thread.

## PAINTED PINE CONES

### YOU WILL NEED

► Pine cones
► Metallic craft paint
► Scissors
► Copper craft foil
► Old ballpoint pen (without ink)

Collect small pine cones, spread on a tray, and leave in a warm place to dry and open. Give each cone a good shake to remove the seeds and spray in the color of your choice using metallic craft paint. Trace the template on page 124 and cut out small name labels from a sheet of copper craft foil. Lay the labels on a soft surface and write on them using an empty pen. Wipe away any ink with a damp cloth and sit a name label in the top of each pine cone.

## HERB WREATHS

### YOU WILL NEED

- ▶ Pliers
- ▶ Soft craft wire
- ▶ Branches of rosemary or ivy
- ▶ Fine beading wire
- ▶ Sprigs of lavender, thyme, or eucalyptus
- ▶ Colored cardboard labels
- ▶ Decorative ribbon
- ▶ Essential oil

Bend small wire heart shapes using a pair of pliers and soft, pliable craft wire. Wrap branches of rosemary or variegated ivy around each heart, securing in place with fine beading wire. Thread little sprigs of lavender, thyme, or eucalyptus through the rosemary as you wrap. To keep these small wreaths looking fresh, make them as close to the occasion as possible, mist with water, and keep cool. Add a small colored name card and tie with a length of decorative ribbon to the back of each chair. As you tie each wreath to the back of the chair, sprinkle with a couple of drops of essential oil to give the reception room a pleasant fragrance. Be careful not to overdo it.

## COLORFUL COOKIES

### YOU WILL NEED

- ▶ Shortbread cookies
- ▶ Frosting
- ▶ Colored candy
- ▶ Cellophane bags
- ▶ Cardboard labels
- ▶ Ribbon bows

Decorate each shortbread cookie with a colorful daisy using icing and colored candy. Allow to dry before wrapping each in a cellophane bag and adding a small cardboard name label and decorative ribbon bow.

## WHEAT AND HEARTS NAME TAG

### YOU WILL NEED

- ► White watercolor paper
- ► Lilac watercolor paint
- ► Paintbrush
- ► Ruler
- ► Gold ink pen
- ► Entwined heart stamp
- ► Embossing ink
- ► Gold embossing powder
- ► Heat gun
- ► Gold spray paint
- ► Two ears of wheat
- ► Scissors
- ► Hole puncher
- ► Narrow pale lilac ribbon

Wash a sheet of watercolor paper with a light coat of lilac paint and leave to dry. Using a ruler to tear against, tear rough rectangles of the paper each measuring about 2 x 4 inches. Outline the torn edges using the gold pen. Stamp a heart at the top of each name tag and sprinkle with the gold embossing powder. Tap off the excess powder and then heat with heat gun to give a gold relief heart. In a well-ventilated room or outside, spray the wheat gold and leave to dry. Trim the stems to approximately 2 inches in length. Punch two holes in each card. Thread with a short length of ribbon and use to tie two ears of wheat neatly together with a bow. Add a name in gold.

## LETTERED LEAVES

### YOU WILL NEED

- ► Large non-waxy leaves
- ► Metallic ink pen
- ► Napkins
- ► Ribbon

Wipe the leaves with a clean damp cloth. Allow to dry. When dry add a name or initial using a metallic gold or silver pen. Roll up a napkin, tie with a ribbon bow, and tuck the leaf underneath.

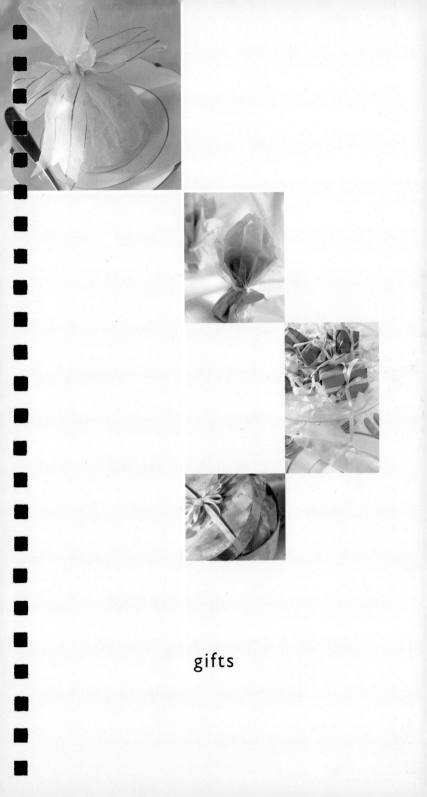

gifts

# MADEIRA CAKE

## YOU WILL NEED

- ▶ 2 sticks of sweet butter, softened
- ▶ 1 cup of superfine sugar
- ▶ Finely grated rind and juice of one large lemon
- ▶ Five medium eggs, beaten
- ▶ 2 cups of all-purpose flour
- ▶ 1½ teaspoons of baking powder
- ▶ ½ teaspoon of salt

Madeira cake is a firm golden sponge cake. It slices well and gives a good base for decorating and frosting.

This recipe makes ten to twelve miniature cakes which should be used as the base for the projects that follow on pages 88 to 95. They should be baked in small 6-fluid ounce metal cake pans, shaped like pudding basins.

Preheat the oven to 325°F. Line the base of each pan with parchment or waxed paper and grease the sides with vegetable oil. Put the butter, sugar, and lemon rind in a bowl and beat well until light and fluffy. Gradually beat in the eggs, beating well between each addition. If the mixture looks as if it is curdling add a little flour as you add the eggs.

Sift the flour, baking powder, and salt into a large bowl and mix well, then fold in using a figure-of-eight motion with a large metal spoon. Repeat with the remaining flour, adding the lemon juice and mixing until the mixture is of a soft dropping consistency. Don't be tempted to beat the mixture otherwise you will beat out the air and the cake will be heavy and solid when cooked.

Spoon the mixture into the prepared pans, level the surface, and cook for 35 to 40 minutes. If you are using a fan oven, adjust the cooking time accordingly. The cakes are done when they are golden, well risen, the center springs back when pressed gently with the fingertips, and a skewer inserted into the center comes out clean.

Remove from the oven and stand on a cooling rack. Allow to cool completely before removing from the pans.

This recipe can also be used to make an 8-inch round cake. If baking a large cake using this method, always double-line the pan with baking parchment or waxed paper, and tie a double thickness of brown paper around the outside of the pan to prevent the outside of the cake cooking much faster than the center. The cake should be cooked for 1 to 1¼ hours, covering the cake with baking parchment or foil if it seems to be overbrowning.

These cakes can be stored for up to 1 week if wrapped in baking parchment or waxed paper and stored in an airtight container. They can be frozen for up to 2 months wrapped in waxed paper and placed inside a polythene bag or in an airtight container. Defrost at room temperature overnight.

# CHOCOLATE CAKE

## YOU WILL NEED

- ▶ 2 sticks of sweet butter, softened
- ▶ 1 cup of superfine sugar
- ▶ 4 medium eggs, beaten
- ▶ 2 cups of all-purpose flour
- ▶ 1 tablespoon of baking powder
- ▶ ¾ teaspoon of salt
- ▶ ½ cup of cocoa powder
- ▶ 6 ounces of semisweet chocolate, melted
- ▶ 1 tablespoon of milk

This rich dark chocolate cake is moist, delicious, and easy to cut.

This recipe makes ten to twelve miniature cakes which should be used as the base for the projects that follow on pages 88 to 95. They should be baked in small 6-fluid ounce metal cake pans, shaped like pudding basins.

Preheat the oven to 350°F. Line the base of each mini cake pan with baking parchment or waxed paper and grease the sides with vegetable oil. Put the butter and sugar, in a bowl and beat well until light and fluffy. Gradually beat in the eggs, beating well between each addition. If the mixture looks like it is curdling, add a little flour as you add the eggs. Sift the flour, baking powder, salt, and cocoa into a large bowl. Add one-third of the flour to the creamed mixture and fold in using a figure-of-eight motion with a large metal spoon. Repeat with the remaining flour, adding the chocolate and milk and mixing until the mixture is a soft dropping consistency. Do not beat the mixture as you will beat out the air and the cake will be heavy and solid when cooked.

Spoon the mixture into the pans and bake for 25 to 30 minutes (if you are using a fan oven, adjust the cooking time accordingly) or until a skewer inserted in the center comes out clean. Stand the pan on a wire rack and allow to cool.

This recipe can also be used to make two round 8-inch layer cakes. Bake the layers for 25 to 30 minutes. See the page 86 for tips on baking, storing, and freezing.

## YOU WILL NEED

(for each miniature cake)

- ▶ 2 teaspoons of apricot preserves
- ▶ Pastry brush
- ▶ Small silver cake board
- ▶ Sharp knife
- ▶ Rolling pin
- ▶ Approximately 4 ounces of white marzipan
- ▶ Confectioner's sugar, for dusting
- ▶ 1 cup of confectioner's sugar, sifted
- ▶ ½ beaten egg white (see warning on page 128)
- ▶ Large metal spoon
- ▶ Round-bladed knife
- ▶ Large white silk flower
- ▶ Scissors
- ▶ 1-foot square of white organza
- ▶ 1 foot white and gold ribbon, 2-inches wide

# WHITE WEDDING

Melt the apricot preserves and brush a little onto the center of each cake board. Trim the top of each cake level and stand upside down on the boards. Thickly brush the outside of each cake with preserves. This helps the marzipan to stick to the cake

Roll out the marzipan on a surface lightly dusted with confectioner's sugar and use to cover each cake, smoothing the paste down the sides and flattening out any large creases. Carefully trim around the base of each cake to neaten.

▲ ◀ Stir the cup of confectioner's sugar into the egg white, beating well until the frosting is smooth and glossy and stiff peaks form. Spoon the frosting over the marzipan and spread out evenly before swirling with a round-bladed knife.

◀ Trim the stalk from the silk flower and sit on top of the cake. Allow the frosting to dry Take the square of organza, sit a cake in the center, draw the sides up around the cake, and secure with a bow.

## YOU WILL NEED

(for each miniature cake)

- ► Small silver cake board
- ► 2 teaspoons of apricot preserves
- ► Pastry brush
- ► Sharp knife
- ► Rolling pin
- ► Approximately 4 ounces of white marzipan
- ► Confectioner's sugar
- ► Approximately 4 ounces of white fondant
- ► 3 feet of pink ribbon, ½-inch wide
- ► Scissors
- ► 1 ounce of pink fondant
- ► Small heart cutter
- ► 1-foot square of cellophane or pink tissue paper
- ► 1 foot of silver ribbon, ½-inch wide

ROMANTIC

# HEARTS AND BOWS

Put the cake onto the board and cover with the marzipan as directed on page 88.

Lightly brush the cake with boiling water. Knead the white fondant and thinly roll out on a surface lightly dusted with confectioner's sugar and use to cover the cake, smoothing and easing out any creases. Trim around the base of the cake to neaten. Wash and dry your hands and lightly rub all over the fondant. This will help to smooth it and give it an attractive "polished" look.

▲ ▶ Cut the pink ribbon into four equal lengths. Push the end of each piece under the edges of the white fondant, equally spaced around the base of the cake. Tie at the top in a double bow.

◀ ▼ Thinly roll out the pink fondant and stamp out 12 to 15 small hearts per cake. Dampen the back of each with a little water and stick to the sides of the cake. Take the square of cellophane, sit the cake in the center, draw the sides up around the cake, and tie with a silver ribbon bow.

## YOU WILL NEED

(for each miniature cake)

- ▶ 2 teaspoons of apricot preserves
- ▶ Pastry brush
- ▶ Small silver cake board
- ▶ Sharp knife
- ▶ Approximately 4 ounces of white marzipan
- ▶ Rolling pin
- ▶ Confectioner's sugar
- ▶ Approximately 4½ ounces of champagne or ivory fondant
- ▶ Small butter mold
- ▶ 1½ ounces of red fondant
- ▶ Scalloped edge cutter
- ▶ Small heart cutter
- ▶ 1-foot square of red gingham fabric
- ▶ Raffia

COUNTRY

# TAKE MY HEART

Place the cake onto the board and cover with the marzipan as directed on page 88.

▼ Lightly brush the cake with boiling water. Knead the champagne fondant. Take approximately ½ ounce of fondant, shape into a smooth flat circle, and press on top of the cake.

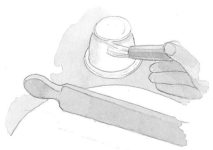

► ◄ Thinly roll out the remaining fondant on a surface lightly dusted with confectioner's sugar and use to cover the cake, smoothing and easing out any creases. Trim around the base of the cake to neaten. Wash and dry your hands and lightly rub all over the fondant. This will help to smooth it and give it an attractive "polished" look. Lightly dust the butter mold with confectioner's sugar and press firmly onto the top of the cake, apply even pressure, and carefully lift away to give an embossed design.

◄ Knead the red fondant and roll out thinly. Cut a strip the same length as the circumference of the cake and 1 inch wide. Cut a scalloped edge, dampen the back of the strip with water, and wrap around the base of the cake.

► Instead of using the small heart cutter as a cutter just press it gently all around the base of the red strip to give an embossed heart design. Take the square of gingham, sit a cake in the center, draw the sides up around the cake, and secure with a raffia bow.

## YOU WILL NEED

(for each miniature cake)

► 2 teaspoons apricot
  preserves
► Pastry brush
► Small silver cake board
► Sharp knife
► Approximately 4 ounces
  of white marzipan
► Confectioner's sugar
► Rolling pin
► Approximately 4 ounces
  of pale yellow fondant
► ½ ounce of white
  fondant
► Large petal cutter
► Small piece yellow
  fondant
► 1-foot square of yellow
  netting or tulle
► Scissors
► 1½ feet of pink
  gingham ribbon,
  1-inch wide

MODERN

# SPRING BLOOM

Place the cake onto the board and cover with the marzipan
as directed on page 88.

Lightly brush the cake with boiling water. Knead the yellow
fondant and thinly roll out on a surface lightly dusted with
confectioner's sugar and use to cover the cake, smoothing
and easing out any creases. Trim around the base of the
cake to neaten. Wash and dry your hands and lightly rub all
over the fondant. This will help to smooth it and give an
attractive "polished" look.

◀ ▼ Roll out the white fondant and stamp out eight petals. Dampen the back of each with water and arrange on the top of the cake in a ring.

▶ Roll the small piece of yellow fondant into a ball, flatten slightly. Score a crisscross design into the top using the tip of a sharp knife. Dampen and place on top of the petals. Wrap a length of ribbon around the base of the cake.

◀ Take the square of netting, sit a cake in the center, draw the sides up around the cake, and secure with a ribbon bow.

# DECORATED
# HAT BOX

## YOU WILL NEED

- ► Large plain hatbox
- ► Newspaper
- ► Pale blue latex paint
- ► Medium paintbrush
- ► Assorted textured papers
- ► Ruler
- ► Glue
- ► Scissors
- ► Silver tissue paper
- ► Silver relief paint
- ► Pale pink cotton fabric
- ► Coordinating ribbon, ½-inch wide

▲ Stand the box on a sheet of newspaper. Give the outside of the box, and the inside and outside of the lid two coats of blue latex paint. Allow to dry.

◄ Tear the textured paper and silver tissue into an assortment of small squares and rectangles. To tear a reasonably straight line lay the ruler on the paper and tear the paper against it.

► Spread glue onto the backs of the paper pieces and randomly place them all over the box, overlapping them slightly but not completely obscuring the blue paint. Cut several different-sized heart shapes from the silver tissue and stick them on the box. Using the relief paint, highlight the edges of some of the panels and hearts. Allow to dry.

▲ Measure the diameter of the box, double it and cut out a circle of fabric with a circumference this size. Turn under a ½-inch hem and press in place. Spread the inside lip of the box with glue. Lay the fabric in the base of the box and up the sides with the turned edge facing down. Ease it into the base and then glue the turned edge just beneath the lip of the box. You will have excess fabric so pleat it slightly as you glue it in place. Cut four pieces of ribbon, each one a few inches longer than the diameter of the lid. Glue them to the underside of the lid, evenly spaced apart. Pull the loose ends to the top of the box and tie in a bow.

# FAVORS

## DECORATED PEBBLES

### YOU WILL NEED

- ► Pebbles, one for each guest
- ► Craft paint
- ► Paintbrush
- ► Glue stick
- ► Faux gold or silver leaf
- ► Rub-down letter transfers
- ► Soft brush
- ► Clear varnish

Collect or buy small smooth pebbles with a relatively flat surface. Wash and dry before painting in the color of your choice using water-based craft paint. Dab a rough square shape of glue on the front, flatter side of each pebble using a solid glue stick. Cut faux gold or silver leaf into small squares and stick a piece to each pebble. Leave overnight to dry then brush over the gold or silver leaf with a soft brush to smooth and remove any unglued leaf. Add a message, name, or initial, using rub-down letter transfers and then protect with varnish.

## OYSTER CANDLES

### YOU WILL NEED

- ► Oyster shells, one for each guest
- ► White household candles
- ► Tweezers

Collect as many empty oyster shells as you have guests. Wash and scrub thoroughly and leave to dry upside down on a tray. Put three or four household white candles in an old metal pot. Sit the pot over a pan of boiling water and heat until the candles have completely melted. Be careful, as the wax will be hot. Carefully lift out the wicks using a pair of tweezers and set aside. Fill each oyster shell with melted wax and allow to cool for 5 minutes, during which time the wax will start to solidify and turn opaque. Before the wax sets completely, cut the wicks into short lengths and carefully push a piece into the center of each candle. Allow to cool completely. Melt the next three or four candles and continue until all the oyster shells have been filled.

## SURPRISE GIFTS

### YOU WILL NEED

- ► Small gift for each guest
- ► Colored paper, enough to wrap the gifts
- ► Pale blue ribbon
- ► Pale pink ribbon
- ► Glass bowl, one for each table
- ► Colored tissue paper, shredded

Wrap each gift in the colored paper. Cut a long length of pale blue ribbon for each male guest and the same in pale pink ribbon for each female guest. Tie each gift with the appropriate colored ribbon. For each table, fill a shallow glass bowl with shredded tissue paper and bury a gift for every table guest in the tissue. Trail a ribbon end to each guest's place.

### FLOWER GARDEN

### YOU WILL NEED

- ► Bulbs or seeds
- ► Corrugated card
- ► Craft knife
- ► Adhesive tape
- ► Tissue paper
- ► Colored paper or cardboard
- ► Growing instructions

Buy flower seeds or bulbs that follow the theme of your wedding: wild flower seeds for a country wedding, crocus, tulip, or narcissi bulbs for a traditional wedding, forget-me-nots for a romantic wedding, or irises for a modern touch. Transfer the template from page 124 onto the corrugated card. Score along the fold lines and tape together to form covers for the seeds or bulbs. Wrap the bulbs or seeds in tissue paper and tuck a package inside each cover before decorating with strips of colored paper or cardboard. Add instructions on how to grow the plants or a picture of the contents. Your guests can plant their gift and remember your wedding when the plants flower the next year. Bulbs also look lovely wrapped in cones of cellophane and tied with ribbon.

## ALMOND POUCH

### YOU WILL NEED

(For each female guest)

- ► Five sugared almonds
- ► Two 8-inch squares of tissue paper
- ► 8-inch square of tulle
- ► 6 inches of ribbon
- ► Heart-shaped labels

It is traditional to give five sugared almonds to every female guest at a wedding meal. The almonds signify wealth, fertility, health, happiness, and long life. Lay the tissue paper squares on top of the tulle, top with five sugared

almonds, draw up the sides, and tie with the ribbon and a coordinating heart-shaped name label.

### SUGARED ALMOND DAISIES

### YOU WILL NEED

(For each female guest)

- ► Small red and yellow cellophane squares
- ► Five sugared almonds
- ► 10 inches of narrow ribbon

Cut five 4-inch squares of red-colored cellophane and one of yellow. Put a sugared almond in the center of each square, draw the cellophane up around the sides of the almond, and twist tightly to form a stem shape. Each covered almond forms a petal of the flower. Arrange five of these to make a daisy shape, place a yellow one in the center, and bind the stems together with narrow ribbon. Secure with a knot and a bow.

memories

## YOU WILL NEED

- ► Photograph album
- ► Ruler and scissors
- ► Medium-weight wadding the same size as the album jacket
- ► Piece of medium-weight white non-stretch fabric, at least twice as large as the album jacket
- ► Iron
- ► Pins
- ► Sewing machine
- ► White thread
- ► Needle and basting thread
- ► Silver sewing thread
- ► Six 5-millimeter diameter pearl beads
- ► Fifty 3-millimeter diameter pearl beads
- ► Two 1-foot lengths of white satin ribbon, 1-inch wide
- ► Clear all-purpose glue

# KEEPSAKE PHOTO ALBUM

Open the album, measure the dimensions of the jacket, and cut out a piece of wadding the same size. Add 3 inches to each of the jacket measurements and cut out a piece of white material to these dimensions (zigzaging or overlocking the edges to prevent them from fraying). Measure the front cover of the album, add 3 inches to the length, and then cut out two pieces of fabric this length, the width being half the width of the cover. Turn under, press, and pin a $\frac{1}{2}$-inch seam allowance down one long edge of each piece of fabric. Using the white thread top-stitch in place using a small straight stitch.

◄ Lay the large piece of fabric face down, place the wadding in the center and pin in position. Using basting thread, sew small running stitches around the edge of the wadding.

Then sew two parallel lines down the center as far apart as the width of the spine of the album. Turn the fabric over. Working on one half, use a ruler, pin diagonal lines from corner to corner, and then diagonal lines halfway between each of these to form a diamond pattern. Baste along these lines and then remove the pins. This is where the work is to be quilted.

► Enlarge or reduce the heart template on page 125 so that it fits inside one of your basted diamond shapes. Pin the paper pattern to the fabric and, using silver thread, sew a line of small running stitches all the way around the edge. Discard the paper template and continue stitching as per the design on page 125. Sew on the beads.

◄ Using a sewing machine and white thread, sew along all the basted lines using a small straight stitch. Remove the basting stitches and discard. Handsew along these sewn lines again using silver thread and a small running stitch.

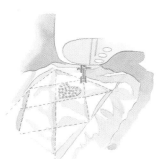

► To assemble the jacket start by laying the cover on the work surface right side up. Lay one of the narrow strips, face down, on top of either end of the cover. Match all raw edges and pin in place, pinning through all thicknesses of fabric. At the halfway point of each long pinned edge, push the end of a piece of ribbon through the seam so it just protrudes beyond the pinned edge. Machine-stitch along the raw edges leaving a 1¼-inch seam allowance. Turn the cover right-side out and slip onto the album to check the fit. Turn inside out again and trim excess fabric from the four straight seams that you have just sewn.

► Turn cover right-side out and slip onto the album. Spread the inside edges of the album with a little glue, and stick the cover to the album. Cut a diagonal at the end of each length of ribbon and close the album with a bow.

# FRAMED DRIED
# BOUQUET

### YOU WILL NEED

- ► Bouquet of fresh flowers
- ► Scissors
- ► Flower press, or blotting paper and heavy books
- ► Picture frame with matting
- ► Paper such as tinted watercolor paper
- ► Blunt spatula
- ► Clear-drying craft glue
- ► Artist's paintbrush
- ► Clean cloth

Dismantle the bouquet and select the blooms. Choose leaves and flowers that are fairly flat and have no bulky centers or stems. Flowers that dry well are violets, pansies, sweetpeas, small carnations, primroses, geraniums, some lilies, forget-me-nots, and cow parsley. If your bouquet contains large flowers such as roses, dismantle the flowers, dry in pieces, and reassemble for the picture.

◄◄ ◄ Trim the stalks short and arrange the flowers facing downward on the pages of the flower press; make sure the flowers do not overlap and lay flowers of the same thickness on the same sheet of paper. Assemble the press and leave the flowers to dry in a warm place. If you don't have a press, arrange the flowers on sheets of blotting paper or any other soft unglazed paper. The paper is there to absorb the moisture as the flowers dry. Cover each sheet with a second sheet of paper and then sandwich these between the pages of heavy hardback books. Weigh the books down with weights or more books and leave to dry. Small flowers will only take a few days to dry whereas larger blooms may take up to two months. Check the progress of your flowers and as the flowers dry further, occasionally tighten the nuts on the press, or add more books.

Dismantle the frame and cut a sheet of paper on which to glue the arrangement. To do this, trace around the piece of wood that is held in place behind the frame. Lay the matting over the paper. This is the area you have to decorate.

◀ ▼ Gather together your dried flowers and decide on a design. The flowers are very fragile so take care when handling; sliding them onto a blunt spatula is the easiest way to move and position them. A spatula will often be supplied with the flower press but if you haven't got one, a round-bladed knife will suffice. Using the glue sparingly, apply a couple of dots to the stem of the flower you wish to glue in place and a single dot of glue to the back of each petal. Position and press down lightly with the tips of your fingers.

Build up the picture working from the background to the foreground and wiping away excess glue as you work. Allow to dry overnight before framing. Dried flowers will fade in time so keep the picture out of direct sunlight.

## YOU WILL NEED

- ► Rectangular box frame
- ► Spray paint in a color of your choice (optional)
- ► Newspaper
- ► Enough thin pale pink cardboard to cut two mattings for your frame
- ► Pencil
- ► Scissors
- ► Craft knife
- ► Cutting mat
- ► Clear-drying craft glue
- ► Wedding memorabilia such as dried flowers, place cards, invitations, sugared almonds etc.
- ► Small paintbrush
- ► Adhesive tape

# KEEPSAKE BOX

▲ Dismantle the box frame. If you have a plain wood frame and would like it to be colored, paint it in a color of your choice. In a well-ventilated area or outside, stand the frame on some newspaper, and following the manufacturer's instructions, use the paint to color the frame. When dry, turn the frame and spray any unpainted areas and leave to dry completely.

◀ Lay the matting on the pink cardboard and draw around it. Cut out the rectangle. To create the heart-shaped border draw a large heart in the center of the pink cardboard rectangle. Leave a border of at least ¼ inch around the edge of the heart. Put the cardboard onto the cutting mat and use a craft knife to cut out the heart shape so that you are left with a hole in the center of the matting.

▶ Using the original matting again as a template, cut out a second rectangle from the pink cardboard. Glue this rectangle to the original matting and leave to dry.

◀ Arrange the memorabilia on the pink matting. Hold the heart-shaped matting over the top and check you can see everything through the heart shape. Using a small paintbrush, glue the items in place. When dry, reassemble the frame. Place the heart-shaped matting directly behind the glass and use the adhesive tape to secure in position to the inside of the box frame.

# FRAMED RIBBON SAMPLER

## YOU WILL NEED

► Frame with matting
► Piece of cross-stitch fabric or open-weave linen, large enough to fit frame
► Scissors
► Embroidery needle
► Basting thread
► Pins
► Embroidery hoop
► Selection of coordinating silk ribbons, ⅛-inch wide
► Clean, dry cloth
► Iron
► Masking tape

▲ Dismantle the frame. Following the shape of the frame's backing, cut a piece of cross-stitch fabric 2 inches larger on all sides.

▶ Mark the center of your fabric by folding it into quarters and sewing along the fold lines using running stitches and basting thread. Lay the matting from the frame on top of the fabric and place two pins at a right angle in each corner. Remove the matting and baste the corner markers. Remove the pins. You will now have an outline of the area to be decorated. Fit fabric into the hoop.

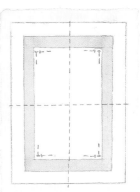

Roughly sketch out your design on a sheet of paper, incorporating the border design on page 125 and your initials and wedding date. Thread the needle with a 1 foot length of ribbon and begin to stitch from the center of the design, starting with the date or initials and ampersand. Sew the numbers and letters in running stitch. The ribbon has a tendency to twist so always keep it as flat and smooth as possible when sewing.

▲ When the letters are completed, move onto the border design starting with the rows of pattern nearest to the letters and numbers. Follow the chart on page 125. With running stitch—sewn in one color—the needle comes up from the back of the fabric, the number of holes in the canvas is counted and then the needle goes back through the fabric. To create a zigzag with buds—using green ribbon, sew the zigzag in running stitch as per the chart. Thread the needle with the second color. Bring the needle up between zigzags, count one diagonal stitch, and then push the needle back through the fabric leaving a little loop of ribbon behind. Leaves and buds—using green ribbon, sew a line of running stitches as per the chart. When complete, go back and add the diagonal stitches at each end to give a small "y" shape. Thread needle with second color and sew a row of "buds" as per zigzag with buds stitch above. Complete the sampler.

▲ Remove the basting stitches and trim away excess fabric from around the edge of the sampler. Cover the sampler with a clean cloth and press lightly with a warm iron. Lay the mount face down. Lay the sampler on the reverse of the mount, face down, and tape in place pulling the fabric taut as you tape. Trim away any loose ends of ribbon, frame, and hang.

## PICTURE FRAME: TRADITIONAL

# WOOD AND MUSIC

### YOU WILL NEED

- ▶ Plain unwaxed or varnished pine frame
- ▶ Newspaper
- ▶ Paintbrush
- ▶ Gold metallic paint
- ▶ Masking tape
- ▶ Sheet music
- ▶ Strong cold tea
- ▶ Instant coffee granules
- ▶ Two-step water-based crackle varnish
- ▶ Old cloth
- ▶ Raw umber oil paint
- ▶ Clean, dry cloth
- ▶ Ruler
- ▶ Craft knife
- ▶ Wood-effect paper

▲ Dismantle the frame and set aside the glass and backing. Lay the frame on a sheet of newspaper and then give all sides (except the back) an even coat of gold paint. Allow to dry, recoating if necessary.

▼ Lay the sheet music on a flat surface and lightly paint with the cold tea. While it is still damp, sprinkle with a few instant coffee granules and then allow to dry. Give the music an even coat of step one crackle varnish, following the manufacturer's instructions. When dry repeat with step two and again allow to dry.

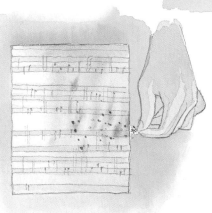

▲ Dip the old cloth in a little raw umber oil paint and gently rub all over the sheet of music. The paint will color the cracks and give the an aged appearance. Polish off with a dry, clean cloth.

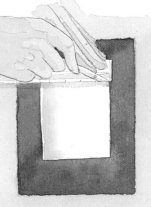

▲ ◄ Measure the photograph and cut an opening in the wood-effect paper. Mount the photograph onto the reverse of the paper. Cut a second opening slightly larger than the first in the sheet music and mount the paper and picture behind this. Reassemble the frame.

## ROMANTIC
# "WITH LOVE" BOX FRAME

### YOU WILL NEED

- ► Plain unwaxed or varnished pine frame
- ► White spray or latex paint
- ► Ruler
- ► Heavy cardboard
- ► Craft knife
- ► All-purpose glue
- ► Wrapping paper or paper printed with your own design
- ► White paper
- ► Tape
- ► Seashells, confetti, flower petals etc.

▼ Dismantle the frame and set aside the glass and backing. Lay the frame on a sheet of newspaper and paint white. Cut two pieces of heavy cardboard that are the same size as the backing. Cut a hole in the center of one that is the same size as your photograph. This will become your border. Set the second piece of cardboard aside. Cut the wrapping paper down to the same size as this border. Spread glue on the border and cover with paper. Turn over and score diagonal lines on the paper from one corner of the hole in the border to the other. Coat the back of the paper with glue and fold the paper through the hole and stick to the back of the border. You should now have a neatly covered border to fit inside your frame.

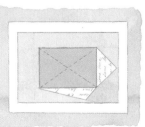

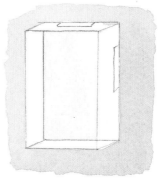

▲ ▶ Measure the dimensions of the hole in the border, add ½ inch to each measurement, and then cut out 1-inch wide strips of card to these dimensions. Tape alternately together end to end, coat with glue, and cover with white paper. Tape the ends together to form a rectangle, stand on the thick cardboard, and draw round the shape. Cut out the card rectangle and tape to the back of the covered strips of card to form a small shallow box.

◀ Apply glue to the back of your picture and stick to the back of the card box. Arrange a few seashells, confetti, or significant memorabilia from your wedding in the base of the box. Don't pile in too much or you will obscure the photograph.

▼ Fit the glass into the frame followed by the paper-covered border. Carefully tape the box to the back of the border. Because of the box, the backing that would have come as part of the frame will no longer fit; this is where the second piece of heavy cardboard comes in. Cut a hole a little larger than the box and then slip this over the box at the back of the frame. Bend over the small metal pins designed to hold the frame together. Screw a small picture hook into each side of the frame, attach picture wire, and hang.

## YOU WILL NEED

- ► Plain unwaxed or varnished pine frame
- ► Newspaper
- ► Lilac latex paint
- ► Paintbrush
- ► Pale blue and pink modeling material
- ► Rolling pin
- ► Small flower cutter about ⅜ inch in diameter (type used in cake decorating)
- ► Cookie sheet
- ► All-purpose glue
- ► Small pearl beads
- ► Matting to fit frame and photograph
- ► Lilac cotton fabric slightly larger than matting
- ► Scissors
- ► Lilac gingham ribbon

# FORGET-ME-NOT FRAME

▲ Dismantle the frame and set aside the glass, backing, and matting. Lay the frame on a sheet of newspaper and then give all sides (except the back) a light coat of lilac paint. Allow to dry, recoating if necessary.

▶ The modeling material can be blended to produce different shades. To make lilac take a little blue and pink and roll thinly on a clean work surface. Fold into quarters and roll out again. Repeat folding and rolling until the material is an even color. Repeat this process until you have four or five different shades of blue, lilac, and pink.

◀ Thinly roll out each color and stamp out flower shapes. Lift onto the cookie sheet and bake in the oven according to the manufactuerer's instructions. When completely cool, glue a pearl bead in the center of each. Randomly glue the small flowers around the frame.

▼ Apply glue to the front of the matting, then lay it on top of the lilac fabric, turn over, and smooth the fabric. Lay face down and push the tip of the scissors through the fabric in the center of the matting's opening. Cut small tabs up to the edge of the matting. Spread glue on the reverse of the matting, fold the fabric to the reverse, and press down. Glue gingham ribbon round the edge of the matting and when dry reassemble the frame.

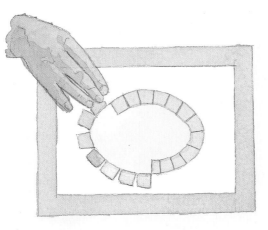

MODERN

# WOVEN RIBBON AND SILVER LEAF

## YOU WILL NEED

► Wooden frame
► Newspaper
► Fine paintbrush
► Metal resin
► Soft paintbrush
► Matting to fit frame and photograph
► Several sheets real or artificial silver leaf
► Iron-on interfacing material
► Scissors and ruler
► Satin ribbons in three coordinating colors, $\frac{1}{2}$- to $\frac{3}{4}$-inch wide
► Iron
► All-purpose glue
► Pins

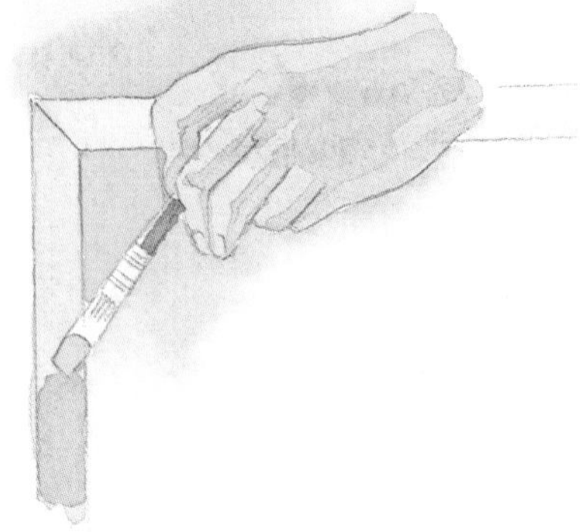

▲ Dismantle the frame and set aside the glass and backing. Lay the frame on a sheet of newspaper and then give all sides (except the back) a light coat of metal resin. Allow to dry for approximately 5 minutes or until touch dry. Wash your hands and lightly talc your fingertips.

► With the tip of a fine paintbrush carefully lift one of the sheets of silver leaf onto the frame and gently press into place with your fingertips. Continue until the entire frame is covered, tearing and repositioning small pieces of silver where necessary. The silver leaf is incredibly fragile so handle carefully and take your time.

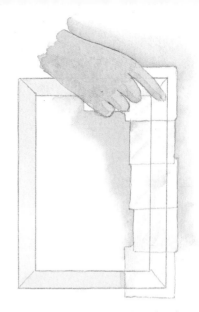

Gently stroke the soft brush over the frame, smoothing the silver leaf into place and brushing away looses pieces of silver. Set the frame aside to dry.

▼ Cut a piece of interfacing slightly larger than the matting and lay on the work surface glue side up. Measure the width of the interfacing and cut the first ribbon into pieces the same length. Lay the ribbon strips side by side on top of the interfacing; pin ribbon ends.

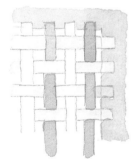

Measure the length of the interfacing and cut a piece of ribbon in the second color. Weave this ribbon in and out of the ribbon strips. Pin ribbon ends. Cut a second strip in the third color and weave this alongside the first strip. Continue weaving until the whole area is covered and none of the interfacing is visible. Cover with a damp cloth and press as per manufacturer's instructions. Remove pins and press again.

► Lay the woven ribbon piece face down. Apply some glue to the front of the matting and then position on top of the interfacing. Press down firmly. Through the matting you will see the interfacing. Cut diagonal lines from one corner of the hole in the matting to the other. Trim off the tips of the interfacing triangles. Spread the back of the matting with glue. Fold the ribbons over the edge of the matting and press down well. When dry reassemble the frame.

# TEMPLATES

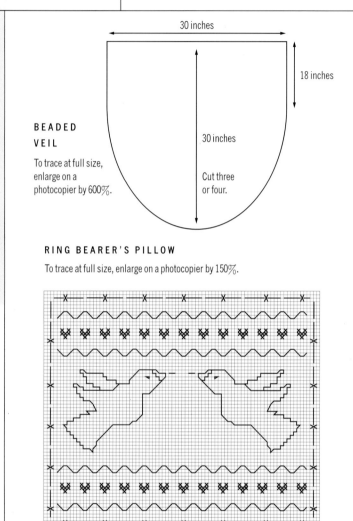

30 inches

18 inches

30 inches

### BEADED VEIL

To trace at full size, enlarge on a photocopier by 600%.

Cut three or four.

### RING BEARER'S PILLOW

To trace at full size, enlarge on a photocopier by 150%.

### DECORATED SHOETREES

To trace at full size, enlarge on a photocopier by 150%.

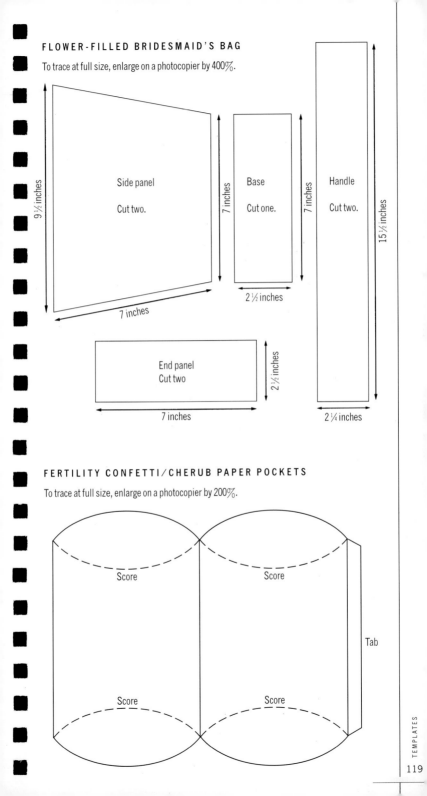

## FLOWER-FILLED BRIDESMAID'S BAG

To trace at full size, enlarge on a photocopier by 400%.

Side panel

Cut two.

9 ½ inches

7 inches

Base

Cut one.

7 inches

2 ½ inches

Handle

Cut two.

15 ½ inches

2 ¼ inches

End panel
Cut two

2 ½ inches

7 inches

## FERTILITY CONFETTI/CHERUB PAPER POCKETS

To trace at full size, enlarge on a photocopier by 200%.

Score

Score

Score

Score

Tab

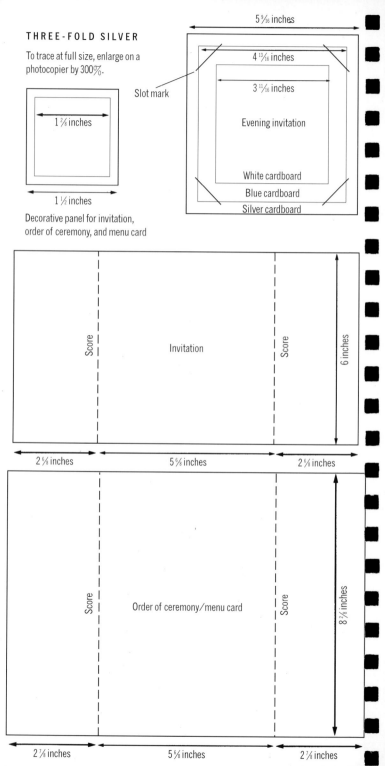

## THREE-FOLD SILVER

To trace at full size, enlarge on a photocopier by 300%.

1 ⅞ inches

1 ½ inches

Decorative panel for invitation, order of ceremony, and menu card

5 ⁹⁄₁₆ inches

4 ¹³⁄₁₆ inches

3 ¹¹⁄₁₆ inches

Slot mark

Evening invitation

White cardboard

Blue cardboard

Silver cardboard

Score

Invitation

Score

6 inches

2 ⅝ inches

5 ⅝ inches

2 ⅝ inches

Score

Order of ceremony/menu card

Score

8 ⅞ inches

2 ⅞ inches

5 ⅝ inches

2 ⅞ inches

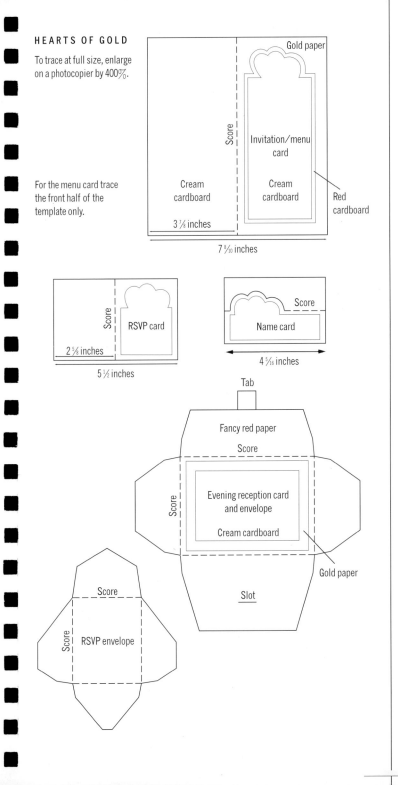

## HEARTS OF GOLD

To trace at full size, enlarge on a photocopier by 400%.

For the menu card trace the front half of the template only.

Gold paper

Score

Invitation/menu card

Cream cardboard

Cream cardboard

Red cardboard

3 ⅞ inches

7 ⁸⁄₁₀ inches

Score

RSVP card

2 ⅝ inches

5 ½ inches

Score

Name card

4 ⁵⁄₁₆ inches

Tab

Fancy red paper

Score

Score

Evening reception card and envelope

Cream cardboard

Gold paper

Slot

Score

Score

RSVP envelope

## PRESSED PETALS PAPER

To trace at full size, enlarge on a photocopier by 250%.

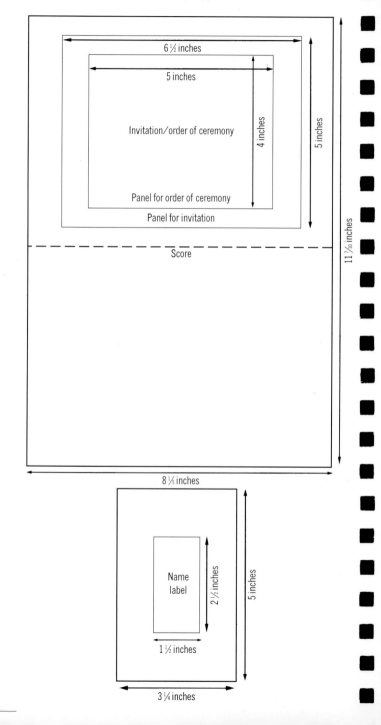

6 ½ inches

5 inches

Invitation/order of ceremony

4 inches

5 inches

Panel for order of ceremony

Panel for invitation

Score

11 7/10 inches

8 ⅛ inches

Name label

2 ½ inches

5 inches

1 ½ inches

3 ¼ inches

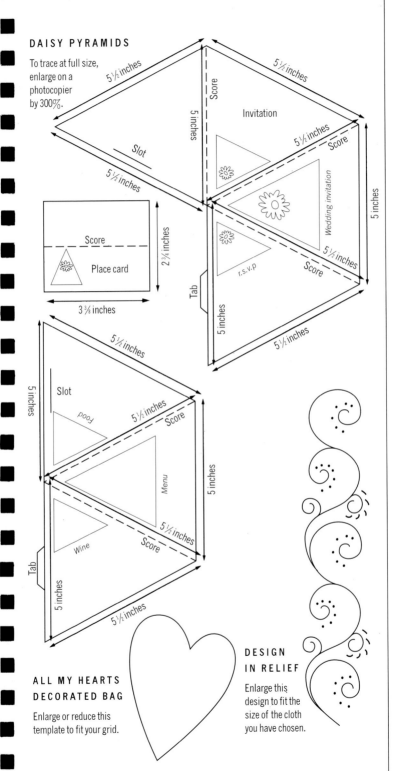

## DAISY PYRAMIDS

To trace at full size, enlarge on a photocopier by 300%.

5 ½ inches

5 ½ inches

Score

5 inches

Invitation

Slot

5 ½ inches

5 ½ inches

Score

Wedding invitation

5 inches

Score

r.s.v.p

5 ½ inches

Tab

5 inches

5 inches

5 ½ inches

Score

2 ¾ inches

Place card

3 ⅜ inches

5 ½ inches

5 inches

Slot

Food

5 ½ inches

Score

Menu

5 inches

5 ½ inches

Score

Wine

Tab

5 inches

5 ½ inches

## ALL MY HEARTS DECORATED BAG

Enlarge or reduce this template to fit your grid.

## DESIGN IN RELIEF

Enlarge this design to fit the size of the cloth you have chosen.

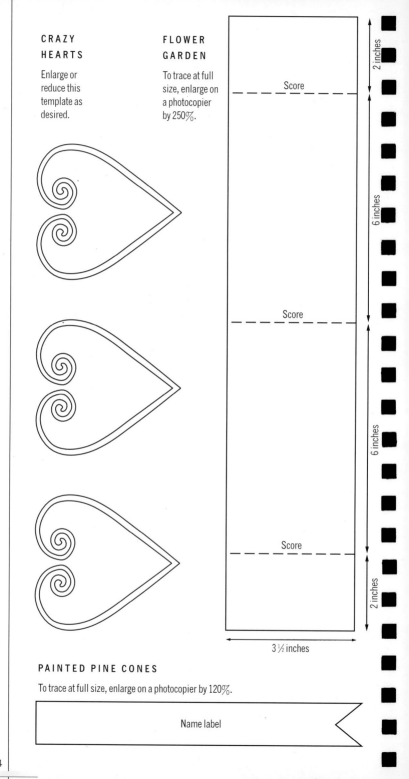

## CRAZY HEARTS

Enlarge or reduce this template as desired.

## FLOWER GARDEN

To trace at full size, enlarge on a photocopier by 250%.

Score

2 inches

6 inches

Score

6 inches

Score

2 inches

3 ½ inches

## PAINTED PINE CONES

To trace at full size, enlarge on a photocopier by 120%.

Name label

## KEEPSAKE PHOTO ALBUM

Enlarge or reduce this template as required.

## FRAMED RIBBON SAMPLER

To trace at full size, enlarge on a photocopier by 160%.

**Acrylic paint** These water-soluble paints come in a range of colors and dry quickly.

**Basting stitches** Loose stitches that are used to hold two pieces of fabric temporarily in position before the piece of work is sewn properly and the basting stitches removed. They take the form of a simple running stitch.

**Basting thread** The thread that is used to sew tacking stitches.

**Beading wire** A very fine wire used for work that involves threading beads. It is available in either a gold or silver finish and can be bought from department stores, specialty bead stores, and craft mail-order catalogs.

**Calyx** The cup-shaped group of leaves around the base of a flower.

**Cross-stitch** This stitch is used on fabrics with an even weave. Bring the needle up through a hole in the fabric, across and back through the material to form a diagonal stitch. Then work a second diagonal stitch on top, to make a single cross. To sew a row of cross-stitches, make a row of diagonal stitches, working from left to right for a horizontal row and top to bottom for a vertical row. Then go back along the row in the opposite direction making crosses.

**Dimensional fabric paint** A craft paint that puffs up to give a raised design when heat is applied. You should follow the manufacturer's guidelines carefully regarding how long to leave it to dry and when you can first launder the material.

**Embossing ink** A slow-drying ink to which embossing powder sticks.

**Embossing powder** A fine powder available in a wide range of colors which melts when heated, to give a smooth, glossy, embossed effect.

**Fabric paint** A paint that, when dry, can be heat-fixed with an iron to give a permanent washable finish.

**Floral foam** For use with cut flowers which must have water to survive. The foam is full of air pockets which fill with water once submerged.

**Florist's tape** This is a tacky, waxy tape that anchors items together. Pull it slightly to stretch it and then wrap it around the items you wish to bind together.

**Florist's wire** This wire enables flower stems and heads to be manipulated and bent and helps to support stems which might be bent or weak. Wires come in different lengths and thicknesses, the term used to denote this is "gauge".

**Gingham** A yarn-dyed cotton cloth, usually woven in stripes, checks, or plaids.

**Hacksaw** A saw for cutting metal, consisting of a narrow, fine-toothed blade held in a frame.

**Handmade paper** This paper has a deckled (rough edge) and natural irregularities.

**Heat gun** A small electrical appliance that gives a controllable blast of hot air.

**Hot glue gun** This is used to apply hot liquid glue. The glue sets on cooling.

**Iron-on interfacing** A stiffening fabric that goes between an outer fabric and lining fabric. It can be sewn or ironed in place.

**Latex paint** These paints are suitable to be used on both large and small areas. Many decorator's merchants sell samples which are ideal if you are painting a small item.

**Matting** The piece of card/paper that is put over a picture before it is inserted into a frame.

**Organza** A thin, stiff, sheer fabric of rayon, silk, cotton, nylon etc.

**Raffia** A useful material that can be used for weaving and tying etc. Available from department stores and craft stores.

**Relief paint** A thick paint that can be piped onto fabric, which when dry gives a raised effect.

**Re-positional adhesive** This makes the back of the stencil tacky so that it will adhere to the surface to be decorated. This prevents any paint from seeping underneath and the stencil can be moved easily.

**Rubber stamp** A stamp, pressed on to an ink pad and used to print letters and shapes etc.

**Running stitch** A small, straight stitch. Pass the needle in and out of the fabric to create a neat regular line of stitching. Keep the stitches small and evenly spaced on both the front and back of the work.

**Scoring** A line lightly drawn with a craft knife that merely breaks the top fibers of the paper and allows a crisp fold to be made.

**Slip stitch** A diagonal stitch that is used to join two pieces of fabric together.

**Stipple** A paint finish made by tapping a stiff brush over a surface.

**Varnish** A preparation used to give a protective glossy, matt, or satin finish to wood, metal and other materials.

**Wadding** A fibrous, soft material used for padding and stuffing.

# CREDITS

Coats Crafts UK
PO Box 22
Linfield
McMullen Road
Darlington
Co. Durham, England
DL1 1YQ

Anchor threads and cross-stitch fabrics.

The English Stamp Company
Worth Matravers
Dorset, England
DH19 3JP
www.englishstamp.com

Rubber stamps and inks.

Mary Jane Vaughn
Fast Flowers
609 Fulham Road
Fulham
London, England
SW6 5UA

Florist (see projects on pages 10–11, 24–31, 34–35, 36–37, 44–45, 48–50, 72–73).

Homecrafts Direct
PO Box 39
Leicester, England
LE1 9BU
e-mail: speccrafts.co.uk

Craft materials.

Offray Ribbon
C M Offray & Son Europe
Roscrea
Co. Tipperary, Ireland

Ribbons.

Pebeo
109 Solent Business Centre
Millbrook Road West
Millbrook
Southampton, England
SO15 0HW

Pebeo deco paints, Setacolor fabric paints, Setasilk silk paints, Gutta, Cerne relief and Porcelaine 150.

The author would like to thank the following for supplying materials; Carol Hook at Clear Communications for Pebeo craft paints and silk painting materials; Christine at Offray Ribbons; Rob Jones at Homecrafts Direct for the assorted craft materials, and The English Stamp Company for rubber stamps and inks.

Special thanks go to the following people: my husband, Richard, whose endless patience and kind help at home allowed me the luxury of time this project required. To Mary Jane, the most talented and accommodating florist I know whose work is always beautiful and inspiring. To Nicky Hoad, for coming to my rescue and designing such lovely items of stationery featured on pages 52–59, and to my mum for her constructive criticism and useful ideas. To Nancy Hamilton, for her last minute assistance. To Clare Hubbard, who is the type of editor every author wants. She's organized, patient, completely professional, and doubles as a model when needs must; you'll see Clare on page 12. To my friends, too numerous to thank personally, whose weddings have helped inspire me to write this book.

Creative Director:
Richard Dewing
Designer:
Ian Hunt
Senior Editor:
Clare Hubbard
Editor:
Anna Bennett
Photographer:
Jon Bouchier
Watercolor illustrations:
Nicola Gregory
Templates:
Joanna Cameron

A QUINTET BOOK

First published in the United States in 2000 by Chronicle Books.

ISBN 0-8118-2552-3

Library of Congress Cataloging-in-Publication Data available.

This book was designed and produced by Quintet Publishing Limited
6 Blundell Street
London N7 9BH

Typeset in Great Britain by
Central Southern Typesetters, Eastbourne
Manufactured in Hong Kong by
Regent Publishing Services Ltd
Printed in Hong Kong by
Sing Cheong Printing, Co. Ltd

Distributed in Canada by
Raincoast Books
8680 Cambie Street
Vancouver, BC V6P 6M9

1 3 5 7 9 10 8 6 4 2

Chronicle Books
85 Second Street
San Francisco, CA 94105

www.chroniclebooks.com

**Publisher's Note**

All statements, information, and advice given in this book regarding methods and
techniques are believed to be true and accurate. The author, copyright holders,
and the publisher cannot accept any liability for errors or omissions.

**Warning**

Because of the risk of salmonella poisoning, raw eggs should not be served
to the very young, the ill or elderly, or to pregnant women.